Now What?

ALSO BY LAURA BERMAN FORTGANG

Living Your Best Life

Take Yourself to the Top

Now What?

90 Days to a
New Life Direction

Laura Berman Fortgang

JEREMY P. TARCHER / PENGUIN
A MEMBER OF PENGUIN GROUP (USA) INC.
NEW YORK

JEREMY P. TARCHER/PENGUIN
Published by the Penguin Group
Penguin Group (USA) Inc., 375 Hudson Street, New York, New York 10014, USA • Penguin Group (Canada), 10 Alcorn Avenue, Toronto, Ontario M4V 3B2, Canada (a division of Pearson Penguin Canada Inc.) • Penguin Books Ltd, 80 Strand, London WC2R 0RL, England • Penguin Ireland, 25 St Stephen's Green, Dublin 2, Ireland (a division of Penguin Books Ltd) • Penguin Group (Australia), 250 Camberwell Road, Camberwell, Victoria 3124, Australia (a division of Pearson Australia Group Pty Ltd) • Penguin Books India Pvt Ltd, 11 Community Centre, Panchsheel Park, New Delhi – 110 017, India • Penguin Group (NZ), Cnr Airborne and Rosedale Roads, Albany, Auckland 1310, New Zealand (a division of Pearson New Zealand Ltd) • Penguin Books (South Africa) (Pty) Ltd, 24 Sturdee Avenue, Rosebank, Johannesburg 2196, South Africa

Penguin Books Ltd, Registered Offices: 80 Strand, London WC2R 0RL, England

First trade paperback edition 2005
Copyright © 2004 by LBF Intercoach, Inc.
Published simultaneously in Canada

Most Tarcher/Penguin books are available at special quantity discounts for bulk purchase for sales promotions, premiums, fund-raising, and educational needs. Special books or book excerpts also can be created to fit specific needs. For details, write Penguin Group (USA) Inc. Special Markets, 375 Hudson Street, New York, NY 10014.

The Library of Congress cataloged the hardcover edition as follows:

Fortgang, Laura Berman.
    Now what? : 90 days to a new life direction / Laura Berman Fortgang.
        p.   cm.
    ISBN 1-58542-321-1 (alk. paper)
    I. Title.
    HQ2037.F67   2004   2003068614
    646.7—dc22
    ISBN 1-58542-413-7 (paperback edition)

Printed in the United States of America
10   9   8   7   6   5

Book design by Lovedog Studio

While the author has made every effort to provide accurate telephone numbers and Internet addresses at the time of publication, neither the publisher nor the author assumes any responsibility for errors, or for changes that occur after publication. Many names and identifying details of the client examples described in this book have been changed to preserve the confidentiality of the coaching relationship.

Dedicated to

Fran Berman, my mom
Thanks for countless hours of listening
as I found my way

And to Maya and Wyatt and Skyler
I promise to do my best to listen as you find yours

Contents

Introduction

*The most exciting breakthrough of the
twenty-first century will not occur because
of technology but because of an expanded
concept of what it means to be human.*

— JOHN NAISBITT,
Futurist and author of *MegaTrends*

Maybe you have been experiencing a change within yourself
over the last few months. Or maybe it's been brewing for a long
time.

Perhaps lately you are finding that doing all the things that humans do — work, relate, compete for social status, succeed wildly
by others' standards, and grind yourself to a raw core to have the
things you think you want — feel like outdated forms of achievement. You may be finding that you like *being* accomplished, but
you don't *feel* good being accomplished anymore. And you may
not be sure how else to go about things, or what else you should
do with your life.

Would you like to have your outside world better reflect your
ideal inner realm? In other words, do you long for peace of mind?

And wouldn't it be nice to stop wondering if there is more you're meant to do?

Tracking the Trend

In more than a dozen years as a career coach and life-satisfaction expert, I have worked with several hundred people firsthand, thousands more in audiences, and helped millions through television, radio, and print media. Most often, they are people who are unsatisfied with the current state of their lives, whether they can articulate that or not. Sometimes outside factors like the economy and downsizing force them to re-evaluate their lives, but other times they are plagued by a more vague malaise, which makes them feel guilty for not being happy. They know their lives are good by society's standards, but they are not happy, and they can't seem to articulate why it is so.

People from all walks of life are in a state of inquiry. For some, there is an inkling of what might be the next step, and for others it is a total mystery. Many have come to me to work on some aspect of their career or life, only to find that the real reason for addressing that aspect is a deeper feeling that they are on the wrong track. What all these people have in common, however, is that they have this yearning now, and that at one point or another, they all say: "I want to do something more meaningful."

As I look back at the time I have spent working with people, the yearning for "more" has undergone a transformation. In the late 80s and early 90s, people's definition of *more* was more money and more status. In the mid- to late 90s, when the economy was stellar, the definition of *more* was to find more time. *Work/life balance* became the buzz. And now, it seems we've come around to recognize that what we wanted all along from "more" was fulfillment: feeling satisfied and finding meaning.

The downward economy, global unrest, and the uncertainty of things since September 11th have caused many a human soul to search for its place of peace. For many, it has meant an upswing in attendance in houses of worship; for others, more time with family; and for others still, a quest for meaningful work. For some, it has meant all three.

"Happiness Is the New Bottom Line." That was the front-page headline in *USA Today*, based on a quote attributed to me. It reflected the shift that my coaching company has seen in this post-9/11 world: less people retreating in fear, and more finding the courage and determination not to let life pass them by. Corporations tightened their purse strings and were less willing to pay for their employees to improve themselves, but the individual employees themselves were more likely to work with life coaches. They were (and still are) eager to take their back-burner dreams and put them on the front of the fire. They are scared, and some wonder if they have lost their mind as they consider outrageous options for their lives outside of what they are used to, but they also have an amazing courage in being willing to take a chance.

The Recent Metamorphosis of Work

I have my own philosophy about what has brought us to this moment in time when we are reinventing how we live and work yet again. I began thinking about it in October of 1987 when the stock market crashed in the United States. I was working as a waitress at the time with nary a hint of my current career, and I remember thinking that as the market corrected itself so would the materialism of the 80s. I thought it was an opportunity for people to get back in touch with themselves after a long high sustained by a phantom reality.

By 1991, the effects of that crash had been evident for some time as corporations shrunk their workforces and hundreds of thousands of people were out of work for longer than they had ever had to be before. Those who were left in companies were doing the work of two or three people and felt it. More people found employment in small businesses that were flexible enough to change quickly and adjust to the times. Many started their own businesses. According to the 1992 Economic Census, small businesses (that is, businesses with fewer than 100 employees) numbered about five million.

By that time, I was training for my current career, and I remember thinking that the corporate decline we were experiencing had less to do with economics and more to do with the collective consciousness of the people who were saying, "I can't do this anymore!" on Monday mornings. When we are not willing to take action ourselves, sometimes life does it for us. Up until this time, there were not many options for what work could look like for the individual, so people were forced to be resourceful and change. And this time, the change was profound. The corporate employees' loyalty was gone because the corporations' loyalty was now gone. Gone were the days of being loyal to one company for a career. Gone were the days of having one career for a lifetime.

This began what I referred to in my first book, *Take Yourself to the Top*, as the Age of Entrepreneurism. If you weren't in business for yourself as a business owner or entrepreneur, then you were in business for yourself as you navigated your career. Being self-employed no longer meant that you were really *unemployed* but trying to look busy. Would-be employers started to wonder what was wrong with you if you stayed at one company more than three to five years, when years earlier that kind of leapfrogging and lack of stability in a resume would have been frowned upon. This is when it became common to hear from employment experts that we might have up to five entirely different careers over the course of our lives.

The 1990s saw better economic times again, and with those better times, a huge shift to a "quality of life" awareness. As the futurist Faith Popcorn had predicted, time was becoming the currency of the era and people wanted to create work that honored their family priorities and outside interests. Corporations realized that in order to retain good people, they had to let them have a life. By this point I had been working as a personal coach for several years, helping people get ahead in their careers as they gave further focus to their quality of life. Just as "getting a life" became more entrenched in our collective consciousness, work changed again.

Even though it makes sense that people today would just be grateful to be employed when so many others are losing their jobs, from my vantage point, I've seen more people ready to do something else with their lives. The shape that work takes in our lives and the place that it holds has become as varied as the individual. People are experimenting with finding what is going to make them happy and in some instances, money has lost its hold on them.

The New Economy or Cosmic Evolution?

Just as I saw the metamorphosis of corporations in the early 90s as less of an economic equation and more as a result of a collective consciousness of beleaguered white-collar workers, I also see this current metamorphosis as a result of our less verbalized needs.

Many people in America, and other countries that have had an immigrant culture, are the descendants of a work ethic that has taken its toll. The immigrant work ethic was that of hard work and sacrifice to provide for one's family. That work ethic is still alive in some ways, but many people are moving beyond it. Our parents and grandparents used that work ethic to give us what we have, but our situation is different today. We can provide for our families, more or less, and as is human nature, we want more.

In her book *The New Culture of Desire*, Melinda Davis says: "[We are] trying to figure out how to live, the last several thousand years of human advancement be damned—because all of the progress we have made so far is about mastering the old world, the physical world, the world we are switching out of." We are evolving past the need to have our lives be "me"-centered. In other words, we are tired of having goals that are just about "making it" and gaining more external proof of our success and existence. Today, we are undergoing a switch from measuring ourselves by external factors such as wealth, fame, public image, and jobs that look good, to evaluating ourselves internally by how we feel, by whether we like who we see in the mirror every day, by what we contribute to our communities and how our work impacts others. We want to feel better and organize the chaos within ourselves. To do so, we are reorienting from a five-sensory existence to a sixth-sensory one. Feeling more connected to the world around us, perhaps becoming more spiritual, including intuition in our decisions, trusting that there is more to life than what our efforts can bring, and looking out beyond the sphere of our own little world are all ways to define what I mean by "sixth-sensory."

Just as man was not conscious of the evolution that led to humans having thumbs, neither is most of our society aware of the evolution that is leading them to long to express who they truly are in their day-to-day existence. Greater numbers of us are starting to make drastic changes in our lives to honor the parts of ourselves we have allowed to be dormant. In doing so, we feel more alive—connected to ourselves and to the world around us. This level of awareness is still not for everyone, but it is for more and more people every day.

It's Not *What* You Do, But *Who* You Get to Be

It has become undeniably clear to me over the last few years, as I continued to work with clients, that career and life satisfaction stem less from what we choose to do for a living, and more from who we get to *be* every day while we are performing those tasks. We want an integration of our work self and our self-self, and the right work (even if it is unpaid) allows us to feel in harmony with ourselves. It is at this point that we equate having more with *being* more and feeling more alive. When we like who we are becoming, it reflects a case of "Which came first? The chicken or the egg?" in that we are also able to *give* more from this place. We experience a richer life when we can embrace this feeling, which for most people has been relegated only to their leisure time or more charitable moments. When this happens, we don't care as much about *what* we are doing. We focus more on *who* we are be-coming. This affords us the ability to dream about things that are bigger than ourselves. This becomes the point at which life feels more meaningful and you become curious (with less worry) about how it might all play out.

Over the last decade or so, this basic human need for meaning has been magnified in importance. It is not always a need we can articulate, however, and it has shown up as a general malaise or as feelings of frustration. Many people may think it's time for a change, but they cannot specifically say why. These are all posi-tive signs that evolution is at work.

As you get yourself on a path to honor this evolution, you are tapping into what I call your Life Blueprint™. Your Life Blue-print is the unique imprint on your soul that helps determine what will make you happiest and most fulfilled. This philosophy is introduced in my second book, *Living Your Best Life,* as part of a process of self-discovery. This book provides you with a concrete and chronological 90-day path to specifically uncover the direc-tion your blueprint indicates for your life.

How to Use This Book

Though most people have come to me over the years longing for clarity about career direction, this book is designed to also un-cover other next steps such as what will follow divorce, separation, loss of a loved one, or relocation. Whether you are employed, un-employed, a young searcher, a midlife searcher, or a retired per-son looking forward to another chapter, this process will work for you. Age is not a factor, as long as you have a deep sense within you that you are meant to contribute more and that greatness still wants to come out of you before your time here is through. True greatness is not tethered only to a deed or career—it encompasses a general ability to communicate with the world from a place of contentment and peace. That is as great a purpose as any.

This book was born out of a conscious decision I made two years ago to exclusively work with clients for 90 days, or roughly three months, at a time (vs. my previous relationships with clients of six months to a year). I had noticed time and again in my work with clients that people could produce extraordinary results when given less time within which to do it, and so I designed the twelve-week program we are about to embark on together. If any given month within this period of three months contains more than four weeks, use the extra few days to focus on any problem spots you encountered over the course of the month.

90 days will sound like a lot of time to some people and not near enough time to others. First, I should tell you that there are no overnight solutions. Some discoveries take time to mature. Then again, you will be surprised at how much you will accomplish in 90 days. Hundreds of people have already made major changes in their lives using this program, and I hope that you too will find that this book helps you discover the next step on your path.

This 90-day program has been effective in more than 90 percent of my clients. Here are some examples:

➤ When Carla started her 90 days, she was on medical leave, dreading going back to work and clueless about a new direction. When she finished the 90 days, she was ready to give notice and pursue a degree in sports psychology.
➤ When Katie started her 90 days, she was hoping to create a plan to cross over from professional stylist to art dealer over the course of the next four years. When she finished her 90

days, she was selling art, planning new buying trips to Cuba, and moving into her new living/gallery loft space.

➤ When Jake started his 90 days, he was disappointed and depressed by his current career, with no particular passions he would have liked to pursue. When he finished his 90 days, he was clear that he wanted to work with children and was putting a two-year plan in place for retraining and getting into a new line of work.

➤ When Jennifer started her 90 days, she was facing mounting debt as she struggled to keep her business and life afloat and wanted to gain new ideas to rebuild her company. When she finished her 90 days, she had enrolled in a seminary after admitting the truth about what she knew deep down was her new direction.

This work takes attention, focus, and self-reflection. There are exercises in every chapter. If you are one of those people who skip the exercises and, despite your best intentions, don't get back to them later, you will cheat yourself. The beta groups that tested this book specifically asked me to tell you that every exercise is crucial, even those that may appear trivial initially. They recommend that you do them all, even if you think they don't apply to you, because you will discover something new about yourself with each exercise.

The steps outlined in this book are meant to be executed in the order in which they appear. Each chapter corresponds to a week, but you can do them faster or slower. You may also decide to carry some of the work forward with you as you go, or revisit a chapter as things change and evolve.

You'll notice that this book is divided into two parts: Naming What "It" Is and Getting There. The first part helps you determine the direction or next moves by asking you to look in unexpected places for answers. The second part gets you into action and helps you redesign your life to accommodate the changes you are thinking of making.

Working with a buddy or a small group, or even joining a Life Blueprint group, for further support (see Appendix Two) will expedite this process and keep you on track. If you enter the process with an open mind and try not to force an outcome, you will be surprised by how well it can work.

If you are one of the people it does not work for, do not fret. Your time will not be wasted. Any insight counts, and finding one's place in life is often a process of trial and error. I know it can be frustrating to feel that answers elude you, but timing is everything and the answers will come eventually. If your "it" does not become clear by the end of Part I, you will find that the exercises for the second forty-five days can be used to further explore what "it" is, although other readers will use this section to forge their new path.

For some of you, the "it" will be a direct hit. You'll know exactly what you need to set out to do or become. For others, the "it" will be an undeniable direction or preference; for still others, "it" may be very clear, strong criteria for what will make you happy, even if you have not chosen a specific direction yet. The results will vary for each individual, but I can promise insights and clarity that will move you forward. With it will come the return of happiness (even if you did not think you ever lost it) and a sense of peace, even if your every question has not yet been answered.

To help you get an early indication of where your blocks to clarity may be, and to prepare you for what's to come, take the following assessment.

Why Can't I Figure This Out?

Being unable to see what's next for you and your life's direction could be a reflection of many different blocks. Answer the questions on this checklist truthfully to find where the blocks may be for you. Mark all the statements that are true for you. Don't fret, because each upcoming chapter is designed to help you through these groups of obstacles to clarity. Each chapter breaks you through to the next. Use this list to help you find where the program will help you most.

A:
True

_____ My life is chaotic and out of control

_____ I have no time for the things I really want to do

_____ I have interpersonal conflicts in my workplace or at home

_____ My home and/or office environment is cluttered and not conducive to good work

_____ I am the sole provider or caretaker of my immediate and/or extended family

B:
True

_____ I have trouble seeing myself doing anything new with my life

_____ I pride myself on my position and reputation

_____ I have put years of investment into my current work or life role

_____ I feel my position or role gives me approval and admiration from those around me

_____ I feel that what I do reflects positively on my family and others around me

C:
True

_____ I have a list of fears and reasons why I can't make a change right now

_____ I perceive negative consequences to making any radical change now

_____ Money fears are a major consideration in my thinking now

_____ I question my ability to do anything else

_____ I worry that my age could get in the way of being able to make a change

D:
True

_____ I feel lost and off track, but can't really say specifically what the problem is

_____ I have a dream (or dreams) that I have yet to fulfill

_____ There are things I used to enjoy and excel at that I don't get to do now

_____ I have a hobby or volunteer interest that I wonder about making into a career

_____ I have a repeating pattern of failures or mishaps in my work and/or relationships

E:
True

_____ I want to do something more meaningful or to feel that life has more meaning for me

_____ People are always telling me I should do or be x, y, or z, but I never really feel motivated to fulfill their expectations

_____ I am not necessarily aware of the impact I have on people and on my community

_____ I wish I knew how I and/or my work fit into the grand scheme of things

_____ I often long to know how I can make a difference in the world

F:
True

_____ I have ideas about what I'd like to do, but I'm not sure how to go about them

_____ I am not exactly sure what would make a job or role satisfying for me

_____ I vacillate between a few future possibilities but have yet to decide on one that suits me

_____ I am not sure if I can find a career that fits my values

_____ I want to be certain before I make a move that it will work out

G:
True

_____ I dread looking at my money situation

_____ I already live beyond my means, and wonder how I could ever support a change

_____ I have been financing a lull in work activity

_____ I do not have a money plan for making a transition

_____ I am convinced that any change would mean a step backward financially

H:
True

_____ I am a realist

_____ I avoid any strategy that is not logical and almost foolproof in its desired outcome

_____ It's hard for me to invest in things I cannot see or touch

_____ I tend to need external proof before trusting someone or something

_____ I take on new ideas slowly

I:
True

_____ I tend to do more for the people around me than they do for me

_____ I find it hard to ask for help

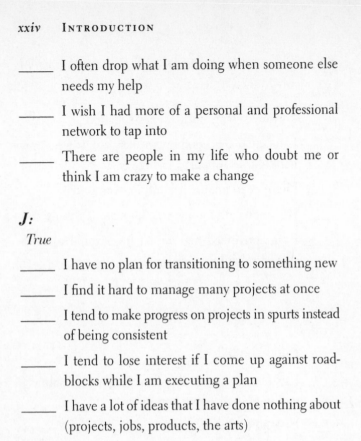

_____ I often drop what I am doing when someone else needs my help

_____ I wish I had more of a personal and professional network to tap into

_____ There are people in my life who doubt me or think I am crazy to make a change

J:
True

_____ I have no plan for transitioning to something new

_____ I find it hard to manage many projects at once

_____ I tend to make progress on projects in spurts instead of being consistent

_____ I tend to lose interest if I come up against road-blocks while I am executing a plan

_____ I have a lot of ideas that I have done nothing about (projects, jobs, products, the arts)

Take note of which sections you scored three or more *True*'s in. Go back to the earliest section where you had three or more positives, and be ready to tackle those obstacles when you arrive at the corresponding place in the program. Using the correlated list below, you can see which chapters will hold the most punch for you in breaking through your blocks to clarity. It is strongly recommended that you do the program in order, but if you feel moved to jump straight into your blocks, do so according to the chapter breakdown below. If you are ever stuck or unclear as you go, back up a chapter or two to make sure you really covered everything.

A: Chapter One—*What You Hate Gives a Name to What You Want*
Getting ahold of your whirlwind life is important to finding what's next.

B: Chapter Two—*With Every Gain, There Is a Loss*
Recognizing that you are not what you do, and finding the permanent attributes you can use to move forward, are critical to your progress.

C: Chapter Three—*Most Limits Are Self-Imposed*
Identifying and working through your self-imposed limits and obstacles will pave the way to more possibilities.

D: Chapter Four—*The Past Holds the Clues to the Future*
There are clues in your life story that you may not be recognizing as strong indicators for your future direction.

E: Chapter Five—*Your Purpose in Life Is Right Under Your Nose*
A sense of purpose will give great context to your life and help ease you into new and satisfying directions.

F: Chapters Six and Seven—*Your Purpose Needs a Vehicle* and *Your Criteria for Happiness: Is This Really "It"?*
Finding a way to bring who you are into what you do is critical to your happiness and satisfaction. These chapters will help you put form and function to your new life.

G: Chapter Eight—*The Bottom Line Is the Bottom Line*
New awareness of your financial life and how it can ease your transition is in order. There is no time like the present to begin.

H: Chapters Nine and Ten—*Life Often Does Imitate Art* and *Put Yourself in Opportunity's Way*

Giving up old ways of achieving and taking big steps to trust yourself, your instincts, and the flow of life are necessary to move you on to new horizons.

I: Chapter Eleven—*You Don't Have to Do It Alone*

The quality of support from the company you keep is crucial to making your transition to something new. You can train those around you to be better supporters. This chapter will show you how.

J: Chapter Twelve—*Following Your Life Blueprint*

Implementation and execution are just as important as innovation. Putting one foot in front of the other and monitoring all your opportunities are key to moving on.

I welcome you to an exciting (and sometimes scary) exploration that will reveal the truth—the truth about what you really want, about who you really are, and about what you are truly capable of. This truth will accelerate your life and spur your personal evolution. You will invite your Life Blueprint to integrate itself into your life, and as a result, you will experience a time of great wonder and unexpected surprises. You will see your way to a new life direction. It will be up to you whether or not you pursue it. However, in my experience, once "it" is undeniably clear, it is virtually impossible to ignore its call.

This book will take you through an encapsulation of the process my clients go through to find out what their next step or steps should be. The goal: a happy life. And to me, that is all that matters.

Part I

Naming What "It" Is

(Weeks 1–7)

What You Hate Gives a Name to What You Want

Problems are only opportunities in work clothes.

— HENRY KAISER

What do you hate? This is strong language for what will be a hopeful and uplifting process of figuring out your life's direction, but the truth is, it is easier to name what we are disgruntled with than what we want—at least in the beginning of this process. Chances are you have lived with your dissatisfaction and it is closer to the surface. That's my reason for bringing up such unpleasantness right away. It actually helps clear the way to a truer, clearer vision for what you *do* want.

Often, we can state what we want through the fog of our disappointments. After all, you are an intelligent, articulate being. However, many of those "wants" turn out to be false wants because they come from a reaction to long-standing frustration. For example: "I just want to make lots of money so I don't have to do this anymore!" or "I'll quit this job and go live by the ocean." Hey, both sound like lovely options, but options created out of exasperation are not always true to your Life Blueprint, and often, as in the money example, they will keep you in a dead-end situation longer, under the pretense that it is a means to an end.

When we are continually frustrated, agitated, disappointed, or even depressed, it is a sign of opposing wills inhabiting our one self. It is a sign that you have veered away from your Life Blueprint for fulfillment. "That's life!" you may say. Yes, that is life for those who aren't willing to embrace the challenge life has presented to them. It has presented the opportunity to change.

Jake was a client who had consulted with me two years prior, but who had not yet been ready to hire me. When he came back, it was because he was finally ready to do something about his frustrations. He worked in the entertainment industry and had been fed up with the status quo for a long time. *But* he had created a nice lifestyle for himself and did not want to disturb his family's stability. (I'm sure many of you are familiar with his "but." It may look just like yours!)

Jake, like many, had been stuck in the same job so long that he barely had any inkling as to what else he might do for a living or what options he had to be happy. He was depressed, and I thought therapy might be a better option for him until we started to talk about what he hated about his job. It was easy to talk about what he hated, so that's where we started. He had great clarity about that, and clarity is the name of this game.

It turned out that the characters and egos around the office were the primary squelchers of his spirit, and the work was dull, too. He had a particularly difficult and inaccessible boss, and the office politics and competition were tiresome. Jake had a flair for drama and, being in entertainment, was used to the idea of a script, so I asked him to write a sitcom about the folks in his office. He had so much fun with this that he worked on it during lunch and breaks as a way to relieve stress on the job. He channeled his energy into the sitcom, and it gave him the power to alter his circumstances, at least in writing. He was also able to lift some of the solutions off the page and put them into practice. By doing so, his fog cleared, his energy began to come back, and he was ready to tackle the exploration of what he *did* want.

Often, being able to name specifically what is wrong or not working can get momentum going and put you into action to start resolving the issues. Give it a try.

> ### ⟩ Exercise: *What Do You Hate?*
>
> If you haven't already, ask yourself what you hate about your current work or life situation. What is most disturbing? Be specific. Avoid generalizations, like "I hate not making enough money." Write instead how much money you are short: "I despise making $4,000 a month short of what would make me comfortable," or "I can't stand having to work past 5:30 every night" instead of saying "the hours stink," or "The place is poorly lit and the politics are overwhelming" versus "The place is rotten." In a life-oriented (vs. work-oriented) situation, you might say, "I want better relationships with my family." A more specific way to say it would be: "I wish I was not afraid to tell my son how I feel" or "I can't stand seeing my daughter only once a month" or "My spouse is not respectful of my opinion."
>
> Make a thorough list. These complaints will make it easier to name what you do want at the end of this chapter.

I Have to Ask

Before we go any further, I have to ask an important question: Do you have some emotional heaviness? Have you been stuck for a very long time in a pattern of yo-yoing—trying to make matters better only to keep slipping back into frustration, malaise, and confusion? If so, there may be factors at work other than not knowing what to do with your life. This often means that it is not time for you to be looking for the next career move or life change at all, and that in fact, you should address the emotional issues you have long been burying. If you work through the book and you find that the answers just do not come, and especially if you are feeling numb or can't seem to strike a discovery that brings you hope and joy, I ask you to be very honest with yourself. Is there something in your past that you have not dealt with? An emotional upheaval, an addiction, a psychological scar, or just some pent-up regrets?

I am not licensed to delve into psychological issues with clients, so I don't. However, I often bump into these issues while trying to help people establish the course of their life. Experience with clients has shown me that truly not being able to grasp the slightest inklings of what would make you happy is often a sign of another blockage.

For example, Pam was a bright, hard-edged businesswoman who had worked in one industry for many, many years. Now in her mid-40s, she had come to me to plot some next steps in her career. She could not imagine giving up all she had invested in her industry and company, although I encouraged her to consider all the possibilities. We did design an ideal job description for her that she felt reasonably secure in fulfilling at her current company once she made a few changes. However, that did not make her happy, really.

We made a list of all the possible things that could interest her, as you will in Chapter Six, and as she researched them, nothing popped her interest and excitement as I had come to expect with clients by that point in the process. I had all the evidence I needed to warrant asking a difficult question.

"Pam, there was no reason for you to tell me, but what have you not told me about your family and your relationship with them?"

"Oh, that I'm an adult child of alcoholics, you mean?" she asked with a hint of sarcasm.

"Have you ever dealt with that? In therapy?"

"Nope."

"I think the time has come."

"Yeah, I think you're right."

After helping her find the proper specialist, we parted ways until a year later. Pam came back—this time, ready to tackle the "what's next?" question again from a place where it was possible to feel the subtleties that allow possibility to shine through. She had excitement, fear, and ideas—all great signs that she was getting in touch with herself again and allowing herself to *feel*. Feeling is a huge ingredient in succeeding at this exploration.

If there are issues in your life, such as unfinished childhood business or unresolved relationships, addictions, or depression, I urge you to begin therapy to clear the slate for a new beginning. It does not have to be long-term therapy, and it doesn't mean there is anything wrong with you or that you are weak. It simply allows your path to become clearer when there are fewer obstacles to it.

The Power of *Now*

We are going to infuse this process of discovery with action in order to create the momentum that accelerates positive change. Restoring order in your home and work environment, admitting to wrongdoing and making relationships right, facing the reality of your money situation, and taking extra-good care of yourself (sleep, water, good food, fun, exercise) are just as important as figuring out what's next. In fact, they may help you gain clarity. Imagine these areas as columns that hold up the coliseum of your life. Strengthen them as you explore the horizon for new directions, and it will feel less stressful to be in flux.

My client, Andrea, illustrates how fixing seemingly small things can help catapult bigger goals. Andrea had just figured out that the road to being financially self-sufficient after her divorce was to dust off her massage therapist's license and grow a list of reliable clientele. She felt overwhelmed as a single mom of three kids who was trying to put one foot in front of the other to start a business.

When she started working with me, we paid attention to the "columns of her coliseum" as we strategized how she would market her services. She needed to attend to some basic organizational matters in her life, like finding a place for her kids' things when they dumped their bags after school, getting reliable babysitters, repairing her car once and for all so it would stop breaking down, and facing the bills that had become the tough financial reality of losing her husband's support. As she took care of these columns, synchronicity started to take place. She massaged a couple that referred her to other friends, her neighbor offered to combine forces with her and co-market their synergistic services, and a local spa finally had an opening for her for part-time work.

Taking care of *now* while you prepare for your new future is very important to this process. Getting things in order makes you feel better immediately. Taking care of these things gives you more power to influence your circumstances. No matter how seemingly small, your energy will improve and your outlook will, too. Please do not underestimate the power of taking care of even one small issue in your life each week as we progress.

> **Exercise:** *Moving from Complaints to Solutions*

Look at your list of things that you hate/are annoyed by. Use the following chart to record the action you need to take to ease the situation, and a projected date by which you will implement a solution. Study the example for ideas. Take care of these items while you explore your life's direction over the next 90 days.

Complaint	Solution	Projected Date of Completion
Commuting to work	Vary my routine: ➤ Avoid peak travel times. ➤ Get off subway sooner and walk 10–15 minutes. ➤ Be pleasant to fellow riders. ➤ Avoid grumps.	Start now
Daily routine	Shift perception: ➤ I have more freedom than I realized.	Immediately

(Continued)

Exercise *(Continued)*

	➤ My nights and weekends are free.	
	➤ Fixed hours give me room to design my schedule.	
Working in an office	Put variety in my day:	By March 30
	➤ Make lunch appointments.	
	➤ Get out of the office 3 times a week to see venues for events, go to conferences.	
Part of job I hate	Do what I'm good at:	By March 2
	➤ Delegate more.	
	➤ Get boring stuff done first.	
	➤ Don't let e-mail pile up.	
	➤ Find more projects I want to be doing, and claim them.	

If you find that some of the items on your list are long-standing houseguests in your life, it would help to brainstorm solutions with other people. If you feel you have tried everything to solve the problem, you have two choices: see if other people can see something that you could not see as a solution, or give it up as a problem altogether (in other words, make peace with it). If you're with me, you'd agree that it sounds easier to let others in with some creative ideas. Try not to judge what they say or respond with "I already tried that." That is just your own resistance to change. Listen to every option, and consider each one a great idea until the real solution makes itself known. Stay open. You may be surprised.

Claire, whose list you saw in the example above, had been feeling that she needed to do something else with her life. However, she had a great job by financial and benefits standards, and she liked and was appreciated by the people she worked with, so she felt hard-pressed to figure out what else to do. She felt stuck and was not particularly happy, even though she had a great husband, job, and home. After putting some specific complaints and solutions down on paper, she began to implement them to find her energy and smile coming back. Her husband and she began to make weekend plans to go away to Paris and the South of France, where she dreamed of having a second home one day. (She lives in London.) She got back to horseback riding, which was a huge passion of hers that she had put aside, and she began to delegate certain tasks at work that she no longer enjoyed. All of it added up to her feeling more optimistic about her life in general and very hopeful that she might figure out what else she'd like to do with her life. You'll read more about her as we go on.

The Biggie: What Do You Want?

Now that you've worked through some of the more harsh feelings, let's see if you can get in touch with what you want. By revisiting the negatives, you have started a process of elimination that will show up again as you work through this book. Deductive reasoning is not such a bad thing. If it's not x or y, then it might be z! We will use what you don't like as a launching pad to what you do want. It helps the truth come forth.

Telling the truth about what you want can be very scary. People often deny what they are harboring inside as a burning desire because they are afraid they will be obligated to make it come true if they speak of it. They are afraid that if they admit it, they may just have to do something about it. There is something we really want that would make us happy, but if we say so, we may have to be responsible for it. And if we don't say it, we get to continue to be unhappy. Aren't we humans incredibly complicated? Logical it isn't, but human it is.

We also do something else as the intricate beings that we are, which I would like you to be aware of as you state what you want. We often put out something we *think* we want because we believe it is a step to what we *really* want. For example, Karen wanted to be a VP in her current company because she saw it as a valuable stepping-stone to having her own business someday. The truth is that she wants her own business, but that is a scary thought. Becoming a VP seems more doable, but it is not her true desire. Granted, sometimes there are prerequisite steps to the dream we most want, but in this case, it's a means to an end, and becoming a VP probably won't make her any more satisfied. She may get a temporary high from being rewarded with the promotion, but the burning desire will still blaze a hole in her heart. Therefore, watch for substitute wants as a way to protect yourself from what you think you can't have. It will usually be harder to gain clarity and succeed in your quest when you put an extra step in front of what you truly want.

It will become clearer as we work to define "it," but for now, let's take a first stab at the truth. Truly, unrealistically speaking, what do you want? (Don't say to become a millionaire, because if you were honest with yourself, you are probably not willing to do what it would really take to become a millionaire.) So again, if you were to tell the truth, what would be an appealing vision of your life one year from now? Who would you be with, and where? What kind of demands would there be on your time? What kind of work (paid or unpaid) would allow you to be who you want to be?

If your answers sound something like:

"I just want to be happy."
"I want stability."
"I want no pressure in my life."
"I want to feel like I make a difference."

here's good news. These desires may not be ultra-specific, but they are specific enough that many activities, jobs, and careers can meet this criteria. Expressing these wants and needs is a great start to figuring "it" out.

If your answers are more specific, like "I want to work on an animal reserve in the Everglades" or "I want a position that allows me to implement strategies," then you are even further along in this process and can even consider going to Part II to start putting your dream into reality.

I'd like to quell any fears you might have at this point about knowing if you really want what you want. In other words, how do you know if what you want is a pipe dream or a romantic fantasy, the reality of which may be very disappointing? You will get a chance to reality-check your desires later. For now, just let them flow. *No editing!*

If you cannot answer the question at all, don't worry. The next several chapters will help you uncover the truth. If you have one of the broader answers, upcoming chapters will crystallize the direction.

> **Questions to Ponder**

What is frustrating about my life right now?

What is frustrating about my work right now?

What and/or whom am I disappointed in right now?

What irks me the most about my situation?

What wear and tear have I endured because of these frustrations?

What am I willing to change?

What do I want?

What do I *really* want?

With Every Gain, There Is a Loss

> *The highest reward for a person's toil is not what they get for it, but what they become by it.*
>
> —JOHN RISKIN

Any change can mean a loss, even if it's for the best. Losing a job, having to relocate, watching your industry shrink, being squeezed out at a high level with few options of where to go, or simply knowing deep down that you can't avoid the truth any longer. These are just a few reasons why you may have come to this exploration, and there are dozens and dozens more. When it happens to you, it can seem catastrophic. There are mortgages to pay and lifestyles to keep up and children to educate and obligations to meet. If there weren't, these things would be inconsequential. It becomes critical, no matter what level of change you will have to endure as you contemplate what's next, to accept the situation and find ways to shift your attitude from loss to opportunity. Every ending is an opportunity for something better. Even a painful divorce or death of a loved one can, in time, become an invitation to grow and give long-forgotten parts of you a chance to see the sun.

In a state of loss, your creativity is down, your senses get numb, and you lack motivation and energy. It's a contagious energy that will be telegraphed to would-be employers, partners, mentors, and supporters, and it will wear you down and limit your possibilities.

An attitude of opportunity, on the other hand, although sometimes difficult to sustain, will breed a higher energy level from you and all you come in contact with. It will move things from hopeless to fruitful, so *please* get on the bandwagon now. This chapter will help. Even if you are in a good frame of mind, this chapter will help you further take stock and revisit what you have in your talent and capabilities arsenal.

Letting Go

Exploring options through the screen of bitterness and anger is virtually impossible. Your judgment is clouded, and everything is colored by your boiling blood. Maybe it would help to know that those feelings are simply a wake-up call, a call to learn more about yourself, and a call to tap the wiser part of yourself.

Many people have been treated unfairly, cheated of their rightful place and compensation, robbed of their sense of trust for contracts and agreements, and have lost their footing as they grappled with how things have changed in our world. You have every reason to be upset when the rug has been pulled out from under you, whether personally or professionally. It's normal for your emotions to be all over the map as you watch the foundation of your belief system and physical life crumble. The beauty of it, however, is that you get to rebuild, and this time, correct any flaws that you had to overlook before. The sooner you can get out of victim mode and into architect mode, the better.

You may be reading this book without having endured a loss and are merely being proactive, as it is now clear that you must make a change. Either way, you can stand to look at how you can quiet your ego, which may be telling you how crazy you are to consider giving up a sure thing, or that you are too old (young, unqualified, or stupid) to start over. This step is about getting in touch with your Life Blueprint buried beneath the set of circumstances that support a lie—a misguided version of what is really true for you. You get the point. Now let's begin.

Moving On

The key to being able to move on is taking the good with you. Take stock of what you can carry forth with you into a new situation—those qualities, skills, and lessons that will serve you indefinitely. What you cannot carry forth with you was just the package those qualities came in. Say good-bye to the package—the clothes, the status, the opinion others have of you, the perks, the bells and whistles, the people that are only there because of the trappings.

You may have formed a whole identity around that package, so you must separate it from the gifts that are inside it. Those are transferable and permanent. The package will always be dispensable. We mistakenly give too much power to the package. The elements to your Life Blueprint are in the permanent pieces.

I spent many years as a professional musical theatre actress and its various forms of supplemental employment. When it became painfully clear that I was not succeeding at the level I wanted and that I could no longer tolerate the lifestyle I had to lead to achieve my goals, I felt like an utter failure. I had failed at my dream. I was inconsolable, and it took me a long time to move on because of my level of disappointment. At the time, I did not have the hindsight I have now and the tools I now use with my clients. I wish I had. At the time, I could not appreciate how much that career had given me.

I marvel now at how many of the skills I honed during those years serve me exceptionally well now. Years of being on stage gave me the ability to speak easily in front of audiences of any size. It gave me the ability to think on my feet and to be flexible when surprises are thrown my way. I've done more radio and TV as an expert than I ever did as an actress, but I give credit to those years for my facility and joy in doing it now. The years of analyzing characters and their motivations as I prepared for a role have helped me immeasurably in working with clients. And the list goes on. Even my ability to multitask, strengthened by years of working as a waitress, serves me incredibly well as a working mother of three children. None of it was a waste, and I hope you will see that for yourself as you work this chapter.

Saying good-bye to the package will be harder than taking stock of your net gain from your experience. The reason for this is that we have culturally learned to attach more value, and inherently, our self-worth, to the package than we have to the growth that came with it. That is why we get so much opposition from the people in our life when we decide to move away from something that seems to be working well for the people who are watching our lives—for example, giving up what looks like a successful career that is in reality making you miserable. You'll hear a lot of noise from naysayers. "How can you give up that big six-figure salary?" "Do you know how many people would kill to have an amazing gig like yours?" "Opportunities like that will never come your way again!"

When I walked away from one of the biggest literary agencies in the country after my first book, they told me I'd never get paid to write again. I was very torn, because the prestige of the agency gave me prestige and bargaining power, but inside, I was miserable. They did not understand me or my work and had no clients that represented who I wanted to be as I grew in my work. They did not listen as I tried to be an active participant in my own career. I moved on to my current agent and have gone on to be paid for two more books, all the while feeling like I had a champion on my side. I took a leap of faith as I invested in the palpable part of what I needed and let go of the good-looking, great-sounding, but ultimately empty package.

Another person who successfully let go of the package is Meryl, a client who wanted to leave an empty marriage but feared the loss of her status in social circles as the spouse of a powerful man. She endured years and years of frustration and sadness because she had created an identity around the package of her rich, influential spouse. It took a lot of therapy, courage, and resolve to accept what would mean the loss of the package and the start of her own meaningful life. She eventually did and, through our work, found a wonderful career being an advocate for people with mental illness. All her contacts and old friends from the marriage became valuable donors to her cause.

Another one of my clients, Thomas, became famous and wildly successful early in his career as an artist. When his star started to fade a bit, it was a source of great frustration and self-doubt for him. It sent him into a series of thwarted attempts to reclaim his place. Once he truly accepted the loss of the package, he was able to move on to interesting, challenging work as the artist he really was. In turn, he again began to receive great notice and appreciation for being a master at his craft.

The package is an illusion; only the parts you can carry forth are real. The package is the past, and what you can bring forward with you is the future. The parts that cannot be taken away by circumstances are the parts we want to take stock of now. Even if you have not lost anything or are not leaving anything right now, consider what it might be like to give up the things you will have to give up to make the change you are contemplating.

Below are examples of what the package and the real part might look like for a lawyer and an executive. Let the examples guide you as you do the exercise below.

LAWYER

EXTERNAL PACKAGE/SHELL	INTERNAL QUALITIES/YOLK
Status	Critical thinker
Impressive education	Great strategist
Money	Flair for drama and showmanship
Win/loss of cases	Eye for fairness and doing the "right" thing
Board position on legal bar	Leadership ability

EXECUTIVE

EXTERNAL PACKAGE/SHELL	INTERNAL QUALITIES/YOLK
Status	Leadership ability
Money	Business acumen
Perks	Negotiation expertise
Power	Understanding behavior based on hierarchy
Leadership	Building relationships
Perceived as knowledgeable	Building teams
In demand in the marketplace	Strategic thinking

> **Exercise:** *Mourn the Package*

Review the next several questions and write down your answers.

What are the permanent pieces that this current/past/soon-to-be past situation gave me?

What are the hard skills I get to keep (technical knowledge and abilities like computer skills, industry expertise, and knowledge of finances)?

What are the soft skills I have gained (personal development, style, attributes like presentation skills, leadership, conflict resolution, and patience)?

What did you learn about yourself thanks to this situation? (I cannot work in chaos; I must have more of a voice to be satisfied; I am not cut out for _____.)

What did you gain, even begrudgingly (how to deal with difficult people, how to withstand adversity, etc.)?

Review all that you are carrying forward with you and answer the following questions.

How do I feel about my "net gain" from this experience?

What do I have to say good-bye to?

Note: If your situation is not about a job or career, but rather a personal relationship or situation, also consider the rewards of having been part of it.

Being the Architect

In the previous exercise, you took stock of your raw materials. It is now time to start creating the foundation to a new life. Your Life Blueprint has gotten its first glimpse of the sun as you begin to remove the package and dust off its debris. You have now cleared the way with a first, small but significant step to creating a truer version of yourself. The key is creating a structure to keep it in your awareness and not letting life take over.

If you are working this program while you are fully engaged in your current career, you will need to create a structure for visiting the process often and keeping it at the forefront of your awareness. If you are in transition (unemployed, separated, or in a gap of any kind), you will especially need to create a routine that keeps you from falling into the pit of self-pity, fear, and obstructed vision.

What I mean by creating a structure or routine is that I want you to literally design your days to support this process.

Some of you may have taken a compensation package as a way to make a transition. Or perhaps you saved some money and are making a change on borrowed time. Maybe you are in flux because of unemployment or another reason that suddenly leaves you with a lot of time on your hands. I have observed many people experience tremendous relief at first to be given full reign over their time again, with fantasies of all the projects they would do or all the relaxation they would drink in with their newfound freedom. I have also seen those same people find themselves losing this newfound joy within four to six weeks because they lack any direction or structure to their days. And yes, there are those of you who will read this and say, "Not me! I can do nothing forever and be very happy." Good for you, but I have seen more people flounder in complete freedom than I've seen make good use of it without some kind of structure.

There is a recovery period needed after a long stint of stressful work or difficult circumstance. Absolutely, take it. Enjoy it. Heal. And please, catch yourself if you feel any drop in energy or state of mind. Most people try to put structure in place once they are already depressed from enduring all their losses. The easier road is to put structure in place before that depression can set in.

I have seen time and time again that there is a surprise disappointment in doing nothing and being needed nowhere. I find this especially true for men, who can often create their whole identity around work. If they find themselves without being needed by a workplace, they can feel very disoriented and often worthless. Many people who have been used to a workplace setting or somewhere where their time was not self-directed, but rather directed by routine, necessary chores, or the timeline of business, will find it drudgery to be self-directed. Many people experience difficulty in suddenly finding themselves isolated from colleagues, friends, or the constant human contact they were used to. Working alone (if you are thinking of starting a business), going back to school, being a student again as you learn something new, and simply feeling like you are starting over or taking a step backward all present losses to contend with. The antidote is structure.

Structure is essentially a schedule or series of activities that will occur daily or weekly. If you are fully engaged in a current career as you explore this, put aside an hour a day for this process, or a certain amount of time every week that will work for you. If you are in transition and have a lot more time on your hands, design your entire day. It's said that you must treat a job search like a job. Whether it will include a job search for you or not, this process must be set up as a daily activity. Decide how many hours a day you will spend on your life-direction discovery process, and then build a great day around it. Keeping yourself active will make all the difference. If you have the luxury of time now, make the most of it. Exercise, schedule time for all the things you missed while you were busier: spending time with friends, visiting museums, enjoying nature, working on home projects—anything that will keep your spirits up and a sense of accomplishment in your midst. Join a club, pick up an old hobby, take on a new interest. Just re-member to make the self-discovery process the priority, and don't use these other structures as an excuse to avoid it. The other ac-tivities are meant to support it, not to distract you or to be used as an avoidance technique.

▶ Exercise: *The Ideal Day*

Take pen to paper and create an ideal daily and weekly schedule. Design a structure that will give you time for the things you *have* to do and the things you *want* to do, including plenty of time for discovering your next step in life and/or work. Include the things that are in your life now, and watch for what you might need to drop or adjust to make the schedule ideal for you and to fit in time for this exploration. For example:

Christopher's ideal day	Karina's ideal day
7 A.M.: wake up	6 A.M.: wake up
9–9:30 A.M.: work out	7:30 A.M.: out of the house, take kids to daycare
10 A.M.–12 P.M.: work on what's next	8:30–9:30 A.M.: attend office meetings or organize
12–1 P.M.: lunch and chores	10 A.M.–12 P.M.: work or other emergencies
2–4 P.M.: afternoon activity	12–1:30 P.M.: lunch outside and work on what's next
4–5 P.M.: make phone calls	2–5 P.M.: work, make phone calls, attend meetings
5 P.M.: start preparing dinner	5–5:30 P.M.: organize to leave
6 P.M.: dinner	6 P.M.: pick up kids
7 P.M.: time with spouse, clean up, do paperwork	7 P.M.: dinner
	7:30 P.M.: clean up, do dishes, homework, bath, bed
	9–10 P.M.: work on what's next, meditate three times/week
	11:30 P.M.: bed

If you are anxious about creating a structure that might dictate your time too rigidly, realize that this schedule is *ideal*, not mandatory. Some days will work better than others, but having this template will help you. Without a structure to support your exploration, it will be very easy for it to fall to the wayside. In turn, the need for it will then resurface when frustration with your situation is mounting, which only makes clarity more difficult. Having a built-in way of checking in with yourself on a daily basis will create progress. Add taking action to that, and the process can be exciting and will start unfolding as if life was beginning to usher you to the answers. When that begins to happen, the intellectual exercise is over and the transition is becoming reality. Daily attention to the process is the key.

One of my clients who started this process was Carla. She started without a clue as to life's next direction, found her "it" within 45 days, and is now actively pursuing "it." You will hear more about her story later. What I want you to know about her now is how putting a structure in place made all the difference to her success.

Carla was on medical leave, and the pressure to figure out what to do with her life was mounting as her date to return to work loomed in the near future. When we began working together, her days had no form. She woke when she wanted to and did a few necessary things during the day, occasionally getting together with a friend or spending time with her spouse when he was home. (He often traveled for business.) Upon being encouraged to set up a daily structure, Carla's first order of business became setting up her home office. She had the space and the furniture, but the space was being used for storage. Once she cleaned it up and organized it, she had a place to call her own and a sort of headquarters for the serious business she had to attend to.

Having the office allowed Carla to have a specific place to do her exploration, which made it more than a casual meditation. She made calls and made a home for all her exercises and exploration from there. Her next step was to have something fun to look forward to every day.

Seeing a friend, going on a date with her husband, going to cultural events—all these things became part of her daily structure. As she put these things in place, her spirits were buoyed and the answers started to come more quickly. In fact, I had assigned her to design what we began to call "delicious days." These days were filled with activities and things that a full-time job's schedule would never allow. Feeling fully engaged in life again, thanks to the structure, Carla found her direction very quickly.

Structure supports your transition. Mourning the losses first helps to create a blank slate, on which you can carefully arrange new choices. Clarity will come. Patience is required, as is insight into the limits you impose on your daydreams for change. The next chapter will help you understand those self-imposed limits.

> ## Questions to Ponder

What do I have to mourn in order to move forward?

What losses have I endured?

What are the permanent qualities, insights, and growth that I have gained from this last chapter of my life?

What is my "net gain" from my last or current position/life situation?

What can I be grateful for now?

What structure can I create that can help me move on?

How much time per day or per week am I willing to give to finding the answer to "What's next?"

Most Limits Are Self-Imposed

*Our doubts are traitors and make us lose
the good we oft might win by fearing to
attempt.*

—WILLIAM SHAKESPEARE

Reasons for why a given change will be hard, difficult, or even impossible are always plentiful, but whose reasons are they? Most of the time, the logical explanation or circumstantial evidence we come up with when confronted with the prospect of change is societal, and doesn't stem from our own personal heart and mind. And these explanations are only true if you let them be true. It becomes your job to disprove logic and naysayers, even if you yourself are the source of both.

Most limits are self-imposed. They may not appear to be, because they are so well integrated into your life that the lines have become blurred. I often joke that cotton is not the fabric of your life—your beliefs are! They are woven so tightly into the fabric of your being that they have become truth. If you can remove them like lint and observe them, you may find they are not really a part of you—rather, they're parasites you've allowed to come along for the ride. They were probably adhered to you by someone else. Parents, teachers, guidance counselors, bosses, the media, and our own assumptions based on what we heard from these people help to form our expectations for ourselves and our lives. Oftentimes, it is also those early messages, experiences, and beliefs that form our opinions and affect decisions that linger in our life later on, despite being outdated and out of alignment with the person we have become.

What tells you you can't? What tells you that the inkling you have as to what's next is only a fantasy? What tells you that the track you are on is not negotiable? What tells you it's pointless to even try?

Identifying the Source

Identifying the source of some of the limiting assumptions you have made is not about blame. It's not about pointing the finger at anyone or anything. Instead, it is about understanding the root of your beliefs. Once you can identify the source, it is easier to re-lease yourself from the grip of the assumption (belief). We believe what we believe because we feel we have overwhelming evidence that it is true. We are always free to choose differently and counter an existing belief with new evidence to the contrary, but it is most effective to find the "aha" that can dissolve the belief into vapor and truly leave room for something new to replace it.

To help, let's look at some of the most common sources that may be harboring your most camouflaged beliefs.

Parents

Now that I am a parent three times over, I take pause in saying that this is a significant source of many limiting beliefs. It is the natural state of mind where children want to please their parents that gives birth to many adult beliefs and limits. Sad, but true. The power that even the best intentions have to leave unwanted scars is significant. Many adults grow up to find that their parents' expectations are the basis for many career and life decisions that just don't fit them anymore.

But this doesn't only apply to careers. If part of your exploration for direction includes divorce or moving out of a relationship, you may be hitting a block because of the beliefs you grew up with about marriage or love.

One of my clients, Andy, grew up in a family where the parents loved each other dearly and the children could not wait to grow up and emulate the relationship their parents had. At 27, he had decided he could not wait any longer and made up his mind that the next person he had a serious relationship with was "the one." He met Darlene, and within a year they were married.

Andy had seen his parents reconcile their differences, sometimes fighting passionately to do so. He saw no problem with doing the same thing in his marriage, because for his parents, reconciling always resulted in the loving couplehood they had. Andy spent more than a decade in a relationship with Darlene, who, because of her family upbringing, really did not have the ability to love Andy as he had dreamed of being loved. Year after year, Andy stayed in the beleaguered relationship, even having a child with Darlene, all the while believing he had to stick with it because his parents would never have given up on each other.

His beliefs made him stubborn and resistant to reality, which caused him years of unnecessary pain. They eventually divorced and he remarried. He was amazed when he finally experienced what it was like to be in a healthy, loving relationship. Previously, he thought he was supposed to stick it out no matter what. Now he realizes that he had to pick the right person in order to make sticking it out viable.

Take a moment and reflect on your longing for clarity in your life. Is there a parental example or mandate that got you here but no longer serves you?

Rebellious Reactions

Many times, we make decisions of huge importance out of a rebellious reaction to a circumstance or situation. Rebellion, a very positive and powerful motivator, can also lead to hidden beliefs that make it difficult to hear your own truest desires down the line. Many people who are looking for their next direction feel painfully stuck because they don't realize that they got where they are, albeit successfully, because of a decision they made years ago out of pain or frustration. My client Feroza is a great example of this.

Feroza came from a strict, traditionalist Muslim family. The expectation for her as a young woman was that she would do as her father dictated, and in her case, her father was physically aggressive and she feared for her safety. Feroza was, at a young age, the target of her father's abuse, but she held on until her college years, when she saw her opportunity to pursue independence.

Looking to create a secure future where she would never need to rely on anyone for money, Feroza pursued a law degree. She made up her mind that as a lawyer, she would have a good income and valuable skills that would fuel her independence. She did just that very successfully for many years. When she made her way to my practice, it was because she was struggling with how she could not reconcile her love of art (something else she had become proficient at and was studying part-time at the university) with law and her need to make money. She really had no idea how to make it all work.

Feroza's decision to become a lawyer was so well entrenched in her beliefs that it registered as the only possibility. When I pointed out to her that there were ways to make money other than law, it was almost a surprise to her. She was so used to looking at making money only through the lens of the decision she made in her youth that it was almost as if I was informing her of a Nobel prize–winning scientific feat. Her whole world had been oriented around that decision, and suddenly the Earth moved on its axis for her as she let that discovery sink in. Suddenly, there was a way out.

As you read this, you might be thinking that it is so obvious and juvenile that she could not see that there were other ways to make money. However, that is how powerful these beliefs can be. It's obvious as you stand outside the beliefs, but when it is you, it is not obvious at all! For Feroza, that fact was buried so deep, she could not see it.

As a result of the sudden breadth of possibilities, Feroza was able to reconcile her creative side with her analytical legal and business side. The dam opened for her, and a huge list of possible future directions and careers poured out, most of them harbingers for a creative entrepreneurial venture. You'll hear more about her story later. For now, use her story to look at when you may have had a rebellious reaction that now serves as a hidden source of a belief or decision that you made long ago.

Cultural Assumptions

A cultural assumption or belief is an idea about what is possible and available to you based on what is culturally acceptable and what has been taught to you. A culture can be a country, a race, a religion, a family, or even a work environment.

I have done a lot of work in the United Kingdom, and I often come up against the cultural assumption that one will not rise above their family or friends without scorn or contempt. People will praise the underdog in the press as they are on their way up, but once the underdog is at the top, they love to tear him down. We do that in America, too, but in America, we tend to thrive on getting ahead of the pack. In many cultures, fearing the contempt of one's cultural group is cause for great self-imposed limits that defy one's dreams and make it difficult to know what the next direction should be.

I was recently fascinated by a documentary I saw about Sidney Poitier, the African-American actor who was best known in the 50s and 60s for his roles in such films as *Guess Who's Coming to Dinner?* and *They Call Me Mister Tibbs.* He was also famous for breaking a lot of the stereotypes of how Hollywood viewed African-Americans both on screen and off.

What was most amazing to me was that because he grew up in the Bahamas in a population that was 90 percent black and came to the States at the age of ten, Poitier had not known that there was an expectation and limit to what he could do or accomplish, according to society. He operated with a great sense of entitlement even though, as a boy, he was even chased by the Ku Klux Klan because of his "disrespect" of society's cultural mores. They were looking for him because he made a delivery for his job to a white woman's home and rang the front doorbell instead of reporting to the back door, as people of his race and "caliber" were expected to do. It did not make sense to him why he should use the back door, especially once the woman was right there in front of him, answering the front doorbell.

His story was inspiring to me in that it was a wonderful illustration of how we must look beyond cultural expectations to find what is possible for our lives. He did not come to the United States with limits on who he could be, and that was critical to his success and his contribution to changing the status quo. Our cultural ties are often much more subtle than those in Poitier's story, so it is critical to observe yourself carefully to find the hidden remnants of your cultural assumptions.

Cojoined Desires

Also very subtle is confusion created by outmoded definitions. There are the old, creaky definitions that we carry with us about what things are and what they mean—definitions that may not match our level of sophistication with other topics that have remained more current in our lives.

For example, one of my clients had defined what it might mean to become a writer. She had a fantasy about what a writer looked like, how she would spend her days, and what kind of challenges she would face. She expressed to me that she was torn between being a writer and having her own business of some sort. Having her own business had a definition in her mind as well, and it was so far away from her definition of being a writer that it was news to her when I said, "Being a writer *is* being in business for yourself. Your product is your writing, and you will still have to sell it and nurture a market for it besides producing it."

In recognizing this, suddenly the conflict was gone and so was the difficult choice to make. They were one in the same, so it left little obstacle to moving forward. Of course, this clarity can be scarier than having a conflict. Once the way is clear, we are faced with the undeniable truth that we have found our way.

Mary Jane, another client of mine, had always dreamed of having a house with a garden, and a husband to share it with. She had associated her desire for the home with having a husband, and for many years, as she went through disappointing relationships, never saw the two dreams as separate, so the house was always put on hold. One year, when her business was doing extremely well, she felt the freedom to allow this dream to come back to the forefront. Through our work, she realized that she could have the house and garden without the man, and she did just that. She moved out of the city to a beautiful spot where she set up a stellar home that her friends loved to visit and a glorious garden in both the front and backyards. She had never been happier, and also began to enjoy the company of many well-to-do suitors that she met in her new community.

In one case, two desires needed to be joined to realize that there was no issue, and in the other case, the desires needed to be separated to be realized. If you are truly torn between two or three options or things you would like to do next, take a closer look and make sure that they are not in essence the same desire or co-joined unnecessarily. They may just be mired in unsuitable definitions that blur the lines about what they truly mean to you as life choices.

Conflicting Desires

In her book *The Circle*, Laura Day points out that having two conflicting desires going on at the same time can make it difficult to make a wish come true. Indeed, conflicting desires disturb clarity and prohibit forward motion in your life. It's as if the two conflicting desires cancel each other out to form a block. The desire to be recognized as a leader in your field and the desire to start a family can act as a deterrent to each other if you believe they are mutually exclusive. The same could be true of the desire to travel and see the world and the desire to have stability and a home. Or the desire to fall in love and the desire to keep your independence. When you have conflicting desires, it is difficult to get anything to happen. The funny thing is that they might not even be opposite desires, but how you interpret them or what you fear can happen makes them appear opposite, which affects your assumptions about what is possible in your life.

If this resonates with you, look closely and deeply, and find the opposing forces that are clouding your vision for the future. The solution is to work out a plan or brainstorm various scenarios that would allow you to have what you most want while honoring the conflicting desire as well. This works as a bridge to possibility. It gives the conflict a path for resolution that will ease up the gridlock in your mind and in your plan of action.

Great things can happen when we reconcile conflicting desires. For example, Cami felt stalled in her career as a journalist, and longed for more prestigious assignments. Getting them would surely mean more travel away from her three children. Having recently been through a divorce, she feared that her occasional absences would affect her children, so she stopped herself from pursuing what she really wanted. With a little encouragement, she sat down and wrote out how she could manage to include both her desire for better work and her desire to provide stability for her kids. It wasn't until she worked it through on paper that she actually got an offer for the kind of assignment she was hoping for. Once she had a plan, she realized there was no better time to take the plunge, accept the offer, and give it a try than the present. She was away three days, the children were with people they knew and loved, and everyone was fine. No biggie. Cami had the satisfaction of a job well done, the financial reward of a higher-end gig, the evidence that her children would be fine, and, in essence, permission to go after what she wanted. Most of the time, the only thing stopping us is ourselves.

Stubborn to the End

So often, simple stubbornness gives birth to self-limiting notions that can stop you dead in your tracks. If you have dug in your heels and are insisting that something is the right direction for you despite being continually disappointed or derailed, you have created your own block to hearing the whispers of the future that are calling you. It's like insisting that your Prince Charming is tall, dark, and handsome, while ignoring the great (but short) guy you've gone out on five dates with. Or being so deeply attached to your job title that you miss wonderful opportunities to grow and prosper because they might mean less prestige for a while. If the thing you are persistent about is meant to be, it will resurface (and succeed) on its own without your help. But in the meantime, a great alternative might just be waiting, and you might be missing it.

There is such a thing as hyperfocusing on a goal or direction, which can squeeze out the natural flow of life that is trying to lead you elsewhere, to an unforeseen source of fulfillment that is even better than you imagined.

When I was pursuing my career in the theatre, I pursued it to the exclusion of all else. With the exception of time spent on jobs to supplement my acting income, I exclusively devoted all my time to my career. I took classes, I marketed myself to agents and casting directors, I produced my own shows when work was scarce, I practiced my audition material, and I did dozens of other activities with tremendous drive and focus that I thought would get me to the goal of being a Broadway success. My discipline and drive were a great source of envy from colleagues, but I was barely more successful than any of them.

My exclusive focus left no time for friends, boyfriends, other interests, family, or relaxation. It eventually led to my temporary physical, mental, and emotional demise, and I can see in hindsight how my goal would have benefited from some balance. It desperately lacked silence, contemplation, and a sensitivity to what life was trying to tell me about my choices.

This also reminds me of all the stories of couples suffering from infertility and spending years on expensive and emotionally draining treatments, only to conceive after they've started the adoption process or given up entirely. Too much focus on one thing makes your vision so narrow that you miss the peripheral clues that are trying to reach you. When you believe that you (and only you) can ultimately control an outcome, you lose the most tremendous asset to any dream—the mysterious power of life wanting to be on your side and provide unexpected opportunities. Check in and see if you ultimately believe any results are entirely up to you. It's time to start shifting that belief. You can give up being stubborn. Start by admitting that you may not have all the answers.

The Payoffs of Ambivalence

A very subtle and tricky block to clarity is ambivalence about a future direction. There are rewards for a lot of people in not having the answers to what would make them happy. As one person who agreed to talk to me about this divulged, "My reward is freedom, not having to be committed to anything, always knowing that I can't be disappointed because I don't care, and I take jobs that allow complete flexibility because I am not invested in them." For as long as I've known this person, she has walked around with a cloud over her right to a joyful life. When you inquired about her life, she always responded with a sigh and the ever-present "It's not really what I want to do, but I just don't know what it is that I do want."

There are often subtle psychological reasons for being ambivalent, which some short-term therapy would help determine. Reasons that have stemmed from childhood, for example, like the idea that being helpless was the only way to get love or attention in your family, or feeling that no one would ever be there to help you if you really could take care of yourself, or having a fear of success because you saw the price your parents paid for having it. If you suspect this is you, do the work to get to the root of it. It's worth it.

No matter how upset it makes you, if there is some reward to the pain of being ambivalent, it will be hard to break through to clarity. The good news is that if you were totally ambivalent, you would not be reading this. So, congratulations. Try to name the payoffs, the rewards, and the benefits of your current state. When you see them more clearly, you may see your way out of the cycle of self-defeating beliefs.

Guilt

Ah, yes, guilt—one emotion that has poisoned many a fine life. Guilt has an indelible way of infiltrating the fabric of your belief system. Even the sound of the word commands that you pause. *Guilt.* It is so powerful that it is no wonder it can stop people from pursuing certain directions or opportunities.

Jill is someone I worked with on my radio show. She had just been promoted in the marketing department of a major beauty product company. The position was created for her in order to keep her on the job. She was really better suited to be promoted to VP, but that role was filled, so they created a director-level job for her, to keep her around until there was room to move her up further. Jill was temporarily happy with the recognition. However, she started to feel frustrated as she quickly experienced the limits of the change she could affect in her new position. We talked about her starting to pursue a position at the VP level at other companies. Guilt instantly overcame her. "I love everyone I work with. How could I do that to them? They are all so great to me, how can I even think of leaving? What kind of person would do that?" she said with a bit of panic in her voice.

I admired Jill's loyalty, and I was happy for her that she was working in an environment that she really enjoyed. However, her resentment was already starting to build, so I suggested that getting a sense of her value in the marketplace would be a good way to measure what she already had with a keener eye. It was interesting that she immediately felt guilty (and she did use those words) when she considered going after what she wanted.

Guilt is often translated into believing we are somehow "bad" or "selfish" if we disrupt the status quo to consider a dream direction for our life. It is a powerful deterrent for many people. It's as if we somehow think we are being altruistic if we put ourselves down for wanting what we want. It's as if we need to state our guilt in order to avoid anyone thinking we would be so audacious as to talk about big changes with confidence and ease. It's as if we have to prove we are a good person.

Changing the vocabulary that surrounds guilt is what is needed to be free of it. Instead of saying you are bad or selfish or a terrible parent or overly ambitious for considering your options, change the language to "I am curious," "I am toying with the idea," "I am considering the pros and cons of . . ." Semantics really can make a difference in how a change makes you feel. New language will highlight new possibility.

As I see it, there is good guilt and there is bad guilt, and possible regrets measure it. Good guilt is trying to tell you that your actions could cause you to have regrets in the future. Bad guilt has no regrets attached to it—just years of expectation or beliefs about what it means to be "good." For example, good guilt would try to tell you that you might regret not making the extra effort to be near your parent as he or she goes through a difficult time. Bad guilt would be all the nonsense that would go through your head and give you a stomachache as you mentally peruse the list of what a "good" son or daughter would do for a parent. ("I really should FedEx a month's worth of meals, send a check to cover her expenses, quit my job to be with her, move her in to live with me," etc.) Now, some of these things may genuinely be what you want to do and may reflect your level of commitment to your parents, but if they are anxiety-producing and make you question your "goodness," you can be pretty sure it's bad guilt, and you're doing a non-productive number on yourself.

Catching the Lie

Now that I've laid out some of the trickier self-imposed limits, I'd like you to try to identify what you allow to get in the way of your next steps to feeling fulfilled. This requires a certain level of attention that may or may not be new for you. You'll need to start noticing what you say in order to catch the lie that you have allowed to become truth.

An assumption is something you've included in your life as the truth, regardless of whether you had proof that it was. You might also think of assumptions and self-imposed limits as data that you program into yourself. If you program it into the system of a computer (your brain), the system cannot measure its truth—the system just does what it is told. This data comes in the form of messages—what you hear or say that enters into the computer of your mind.

Catch yourself as you begin to verbally commit your beliefs about yourself or your circumstances to truth. Sometimes it is a subtle statement; other times, it is a loud complaint you repeat over and over again to anyone who will listen. In other words, as you tell your story about your current situation, pay attention to where you editorialize or exaggerate the truth for dramatic effect. Even if you are known for your devil-may-care attitude or your humorous approach to life, be aware that the things you say to trivialize your pain may really just be a defense mechanism so you can avoid trying something new. It is also easy to repeat a funny story over and over and start to believe it as fact instead of fiction.

If you absolutely cannot identify the things you say that reveal nonproductive thinking, ask your closest friends and family members to start listening for the things you say that cut you or your possibilities down. For example, if you describe being downsized as, "Well, hey they had to blame someone, so it might as well be me," you are, in essence, assuming that the decision was personal and that you somehow did something to deserve being let go. You may have meant it as a joke, as a lighthearted way to accept your plight, but there is more ammunition in that statement than you give yourself credit for. Or how about this example: "At my age, it will be a miracle to find something as lucrative as what I did before." It is easy to believe that statement as fact, since we have seen that exact thing happen to many people, but making it a fact limits you. I am not suggesting denial, but I am suggesting using the truth to your benefit instead of to your limitation.

▶ **Exercise:** *Assessing the Negatives*

Take pen to paper and write down all the negative messages you hear yourself repeating in your mind or to others as you try to get at your life's next direction. Also write down those messages that you remember hearing at other times in your life, either from your mouth or somebody else's. See the example below.

Message	Source	Assumption
(What you say)	(Who said it first)	(What you believe)
I can't *do* that	Father always said self-employed people were jobless folks with good sales skills	People need proper training and degrees to have a business
My type of person doesn't prosper	Mother always said know your station in life and all will be fine	I am stuck
I'm different; things will never apply to me	A teacher used to single me out and say I had bad luck and was a bad apple	Things don't work for me like they do for other people

Pulling the Lint from the Fabric of Your Life: Your Beliefs

We've spent time trying to root out the hidden beliefs that may be holding you back from moving your life forward, but now it is time to do something about them. It can help to know where they came from, but that is not a prerequisite for being free of them. Ultimately, what is most important is to work your way through your beliefs, around them, or over them. Just getting them to serve you well is the point.

For the record, in case you haven't noticed, I don't necessarily believe in positive thinking. I do, however, believe in productive thinking. Is it productive to believe that you take longer than most to find their way? No. So stop. Stop now!

Is it productive to believe you can't have what others have because you had a questionable background? No. Well, stop!

Is it productive to think that the boss hates you despite all the evidence you have that it isn't true? *No!* So please cut it out!

Coming out from under the negative or counterproductive beliefs you have is the matter at hand. Now is the time to learn how to pull it all apart to find the culprit that gets in your way and to do something about it once and for all. Now is the time to bring your Life Blueprint further into focus.

Here are four simple steps to reversing any doubts or fears that are limiting your ability to find your life's most current direction. All they require is three minutes, a piece of paper and pencil, and a commitment to take action once you've broken through to the other side. You can use the exercise on page 46 to go through the steps. Here are the four steps:

1. Name it.
2. Examine the evidence.
3. Shift it.
4. Cement it.

Name it.

You did this in the previous exercise. Name the belief or assumption you operate under as truth. State it clearly and specifically. What is it that you say to yourself, repeat to others, or simply state in your mind that has become your basic operating assumption? Write it down.

Examine the evidence.

Now, list all the evidence you have that this belief or assumption is true. The only reason why this assumption is in your life is because you have evidence that backs it up. You did not just suddenly decide that you are dumb. Something happened and got reinforced several times, which led you to believe it was true. That is the evidence—those events or statements or significant moments that cemented the misplaced truth.

For example, Frank had trouble believing he was worth more in the workplace because he always believed he was a little slow in gaining speed at his job. He had evidence of his slowness that stemmed from grade school, so he assumed he'd always have to deal with how he felt and what he would be worth in the market.

Shift it.

Once you've identified the belief or assumption, and the evidence that supports it, you have to dissect it in order to shift out of its hold on you. Every belief you hold dear presents you with a choice. You can make it truth or you can choose not to believe it. Those of highly analytical and logical capabilities will find this very hard. You have so much empirical evidence to back up what you believe is true that choosing otherwise will feel like New-Age fluff.

There are two ways that I will ask you to look at your assumption to break its grip on you. They both begin as mental exercises, but our fourth step, "Cement it," will make them a reality. Examine your assumption through the lens of it being productive vs. counterproductive and possible vs. probable.

Ask yourself: "Is believing this assumption getting me where I want to go?" In other words, is it productive to operate from this assumption? Probably not. Is it productive to believe you are too old to make a change? Does it get you anywhere to believe you're too far past the dating years to look for love again? Is it productive to believe that you are too young to be taken seriously in your own business? Is it productive to believe your lack of training makes you any less talented? If it is not productive, choose to believe differently.

I am not suggesting that there are not steps you will have to take to meet certain requirements of a new field or a situation you want to be in, but I am suggesting that believing you can't do something before you have even really given it your all is counterproductive. Reality will smack you in the face without your help, thank you. If there is something real to overcome (for example, if you cannot get a position as a technician without a certificate), you'll know. But, there is no sense in stopping yourself when you don't really have to.

Once you've answered that question, in order to help you dissolve it further, look at it again through the lens of possibility vs. probability. This book is not about probability, but rather possibility. Something can be possible even if it is not probable. When man dreamed of putting humans into space, he had to believe it was possible, although in its early stages, without any know-how, it was not probable. So forget statistics, proof, and probability. You have to invest in what is possible. That is how change can occur. That is how a new direction can be revealed. It is how you get unstuck.

Write down what is probable about what you believe and what is possible if you stop believing in your limits.

At 29 years old (but looking more like 25), I started knocking on corporations' doors to introduce coaching. I assumed I was too young and inexperienced to get anyone to take me seriously, and that was exactly what happened. When I chose to be more productive in my thinking, and stopped projecting the lack of confidence this belief had infused in me, I started to get yeses. It gave me more possibilities and ideas as to how to infiltrate the market I had chosen, and I found several successful back doors into the companies I wanted contracts from.

You have to make it possible, at least in your mind. Put the productive belief fully on your radar screen, and start behaving differently because of it. What you think determines what you are willing to do. And when you are redirecting your life (or trying to include the redirection that is happening without your consent!), you have to be willing to swing far out of your comfort zone. Anything is possible, and that needs to be your mantra as you continue through this book.

Cement it.

Most people need some evidence to feel encouraged to do something different or new. The evidence that your direction is possible can be found by looking around and finding examples of people who have done something similar. You need role models.

Write down people who you know or have heard of that have accomplished something by thinking the way you need to think. You can also use your own prior positive experiences as evidence of what is possible. Think of times you did do things that worked out very well.

The greatest evidence, however, that will cement your more productive beliefs is your own action. Take action. Start doing things or talking to people or getting out and exploring other options, and garner your own evidence that what you have decided is possible and can become reality.

My husband recently shifted the direction of his business and went from being an award-winning television commercial producer to a producer of personal documentaries and tributes. He left the "big bucks" to find more soul to his work during a downward economy, and he had to believe it was possible—or else what was the point? In doing so, he made umpteen phone calls to old colleagues and acquaintances to inform them of the change in direction he was pursuing. The feedback was positive, and it fueled him to stay the course. It took a year to change the tides, but the early indicators gave him the evidence that he was on the right track.

> **Exercise:** *Break Through Limits*

Try the formula by filling in the blanks.

Name it: My belief or assumption is _____

_____

Examine the evidence: I know it is true because _____

_____

(Continued)

Exercise *(Continued)*

Shift it: Is it productive to believe this? _____

_____

It would be more productive to believe _____

_____

What is probable is _____

_____

What is possible is _____

_____

Cement it: What models do I have that this is possible?

_____

What action can I take to create my own evidence and conviction? List them below.

1. _____

2. _____

3. _____

4. _____

5. _____

Sondra had always had an underlying belief that she was stupid. It originated in high school, when a teacher suggested that she would never pass a certain entrance exam. She had accumulated plenty of evidence in her life—instances when she could argue that she really might be stupid. It was a well-integrated belief; it was a part of the fabric of her life. When she put that belief under the microscope, as you did in the last exercise, she shifted her focus to what would be possible if she chose to believe differently. She felt more courageous about considering a job change once she focused on collecting evidence that she was smart and capable.

She determined that she could stop apologizing when she didn't have to or truly mean to, and she could stop using self-deprecating humor. She also saw how she could stand to practice taking compliments graciously. All of these were ways to take action toward giving up the notion that she was stupid. As she did this, more and more ideas and directions for her life started to bubble up and get her attention. By moving into a frame of mind that allowed change to be possible, her creativity kicked in and she got excited about how her life could change. She began to see that maybe she was not stupid after all.

Fear

I have been asked many times over the last few years why my books and my speeches make very little mention of fear, if any. It's a realization that makes me chuckle, because I guide people through their fears and blocks every day, and I have my own. The reason I don't pay a lot of attention to fear is that I view it as a fact of life—fear is there and will always be there. I simply take it for granted, but that's not as negative or hopeless as it may sound. Where I come from, fear is a given. We are not victorious over fear by eradicating it completely and becoming fearless, but rather, by lessening the amount of room we give fear in our life. When we improve our relationship with fear, we succeed.

When fear is your master and you shrink at its presence, you experience fear as a paralyzing force. When you are the master and fear is an annoyance that occasionally distracts you, you have transformed yourself and your circumstances. Will fear be a serious disease that takes over your life, or will it be like the common cold, which throws you off for a while but doesn't really change you?

I used to experience fear as a menace that tried to rule my life. Then, I felt it was a constant companion that was waiting for me to fall down so it could be the boss again. Later, it was a companion that I'd grown sick of, but allowed to stay because of our comfort with each other. Presently, fear is a distant relative that visits at the most inopportune times, but I know how to handle it with polite interaction and an invitation to go on its merry way.

It's always easier to recognize fear when others are suffering from it. It's harder to recognize it in yourself. Sometimes fear just sounds like reason and logic.

The famous work on psycho-spiritual transformation, *A Course in Miracles*, says every thought is either rooted in fear or rooted in love. You choose which way to see things rather than orienting your thoughts around whichever way crops up. It can still be tricky to tell the difference, but I can almost guarantee that if a line of thinking causes you pain, it is based in fear. Let me make the distinction for you. In pain? Running on fear. Easing up and feeling hopeful (even if your heart is still racing and your pulse is up)? Love. Yup, love.

When fear is something you can embrace, or at least sit next to in silence as you would a stranger on a park bench, you will be free to move forward.

▶ Questions to Ponder

What assumptions do I operate under that hold me back?

What source can I attribute them to?

What have I learned about myself as a result of this chapter?

What do I hold true that is counterproductive?

What can I hold true that is more productive?

What is possible for me?

What action do I need to take to cement this possibility?

What am I afraid of? What do I allow to stop me, even after the discoveries I've made in this chapter?

The Past Holds the Clues to the Future

> *He who controls the past commands the future. He who commands the future conquers the past.*
>
> —GEORGE ORWELL

By now, there should be some clouds parting over your road to clarity. You may be itching to get to the *doing*—making your new-found insights some sort of reality. If you've figured "it" out and are ready to take action toward a new direction, you can jump ahead, but there is also value in staying here to look at your discoveries through another lens. Each chapter will reveal more. The rest of us will be right here, continuing our excavation for clues as to our future direction.

Oddly enough, to determine the future course, we are going to review the course you have traveled in the past. The past holds many clues as to what you are meant to be doing now and where you might have gotten off track from your Life Blueprint. As I said earlier, nothing we have done in the past is a waste, and it all happened for good reason. Where would you be without your life story to tell? However, your Life Blueprint is your core, which will be more at peace when you are being true to it, and you'll want to rediscover it to get on the path to feeling fulfilled.

Scanning the past for clues is not foreign to most of us. Every time you've had to rewrite your résumé or figure out what your strengths are or what might be the logical next step in your life or career, you have checked in with what you've done before. This time, however, we will not be analyzing the past in terms of *what* you've done. You will not concern yourself with *what* strengths you have, *what* positions you've held, *what* roles you've played, but instead you will start focusing your attention on *who* you have been and *where* you have the opportunities to feel free to shine the better parts of yourself. I said early on that satisfaction does not stem from *what* we do, but from *who* we get to be while we are doing it. As we scan the past for clues, keep a special sensitivity attuned to the qualities you get to express and embody (or did in the past) as you worked or enjoyed certain aspects of your life.

Your Story and Your Résumé

A technique I adopted early on in my practice was asking my clients for a personal history at the outset of our working together. So many times, things that clients would write off as insignificant in their life, or that they might never have mentioned to me, become major clues to the future, so getting them to share a scan of their past right up front became invaluable.

Significant moments in your personal history might reflect your future direction. So many times, there are things that you've had to reconcile or blow off as being insignificant that really are gems that could light your way to the future. Carla, who you heard about briefly when we explored a structure for this journey in Chapter Two, had a huge gem she would not have told me about if I had not asked her to write me her personal history.

Carla, who was in her early 30s, took advantage of a medical leave from her job at an office furniture company to figure out what she would like to do with her life. She dreaded going back to work, and as each day pressed on, she felt more and more pressured to discover the answer to what she should do. She said she had no idea what to expect from working with me and that she had absolutely no clue as to what she wanted to do, but she was drawn to the process nonetheless.

Within 45 days, and spanning four sessions, we had found the new direction for her life. She was shocked and kind of scared that it had happened so fast. For her, the clue to her future direction was in the past. It was the first exercise that we did—chronicling her life story in bullet points—and there it was rather early on: ten years as a champion gymnast. Carla had been a champion headed for the Olympics, when an injury ended her career. She says she mourned it and moved on, finished college, got married, and got a job.

What I saw—and what she came to recognize later—was that this was a significant piece of her past life that was not reflected in any way in her current situation. It didn't even matter that she was not on an athletic field; what did matter was that a former champion was settling for less than a champion's shot at life. Once Carla moved through the first 45 days of exploration, she could no longer deny that sports had to be a part of her life.

Too old to get back to professional competition, not interested in coaching young athletes, and not willing to be a physical education teacher, Carla did not immediately see a possible connection between the past and the present. However, through the coaching process, she found that being on a path that headed to a degree in sports psychology was the direction that called to her. Carla's new goal was to work with athletes on performance and dealing with the stress of their lifestyle, as well as helping them transition to other careers, as it became appropriate.

Carla returned to her job after her medical leave, only to quit within a few weeks in order to devote herself full-time to her retraining. She and her husband sat down and worked out how they could live without her income. Some of her savings would pay for her classes, but otherwise, they decided where they could cut back and live off what he made. Carla began to get more involved in her community, where she wanted to try her hand at public speaking, addressing high-school athletes on what she learned from being a champion. After the 90-day process, she was clear on her new direction and had a plan in hand for a transition to her new life. Her future direction took on a momentum of its own once we struck gold with this one detail from her past.

> ### Exercise: *Your Personal History*

Put pen to paper and take a journey from the past to the present. Start from the beginning and document your life. Use bullet points instead of writing prose to document your personal history. For example, instead of writing "I was born on a farm in rural Arkansas. By the time I was born, my parents divorced, so I was left to be raised by my grandmother," you would write:

1963

> ➤ Born on farm, rural Arkansas
> ➤ Parents divorced at birth
> ➤ Raised by Grandma

Bullets will allow things to jump off the page at you later, when you are looking for themes and clues that could lead to a future direction. Include significant accomplishments from as far back as you can remember, and also jobs and roles you filled throughout your life. Include loves, hobbies, and experiences that formed you: moving, divorces, births, job changes, challenges, milestones, achievements — they are all part of your personal history.

When you are done, read it through, absorb each stage, and start looking for the clues that I describe throughout this chapter.

Now, I would not be surprised if you told me that there was nothing significant that stood out for you in looking at your personal history. In my experience, most people find the standout moments, but those of you who do not may simply be suffering from the "oh, it's just my life" syndrome. It's not a real syndrome, just my pet name for when we don't recognize our own accomplishments. If that is you, a second round of bullet points might be useful. Look for less concrete events and more fleeting experiences that were enjoyable or meaningful. What did you want to be when you grew up? What kind of activities drew your attention through the years? What kind of people always fascinated you? Anything else you can add will help.

You might also engage someone else in this exercise with you. Have them read over your personal history and point out the things that seem significant or watch for what interests them in your history, and you'll find the spots that are impressive and unusual. Everyone has a Life Blueprint, and even if it is deeply buried or disguised, it will start to show up as you track your personal history.

Identifying the Clues

When I read my clients' personal histories, I often feel like I am interpreting tea leaves. I can see the clues jump out at me. I can see which directions a person may consider, or I may see a theme to their life that indicates something significant, or a motivation in their life that may have been born in the past but no longer serves them today. Things jump from the page to fuel the questions that I will ask my clients to further chip away at the truth behind their desires. Here, I will guide you through doing this for yourself.

There are three predominant clues that have come to my attention as the sources that can help you gain more clarity for the direction and decisions in your life. They are: golden threads, interrupted dreams, and driving motivators. Try to be objective, if possible, while you scan your story, and determine if you see the following clues.

Golden Threads

A *golden thread* is a through-line or theme that jells in the context of your story. There can be several, so look to see if you find any major themes in your personal history: an interest that has followed you through your life, an entrepreneurial spirit, a through-line to the kind of jobs you've held (for example, if they are all in sales or all in artistic forums), or a tendency toward a certain role, perhaps as a leader or administrator or anything that seems to reappear in different guises. In other words, the themes can show up as preferences, roles, interests, callings, causes, cultures, status, or environments.

Even certain patterns in behavior can run as a golden thread through your history. For example, you might see that you left jobs or relationships just as they got challenging or just before you got to the pinnacle of them, or perhaps a pattern of having difficulty with transitions in your life that result in staying with the "safe" bet.

Steve was doing just that. It wasn't until he saw it in his history—right there, undeniably recorded in front of him—that he recognized the reason he could not see what was next for him in his life. He saw that he would push all notions of other directions or interests out of his mind in order to stay with what he already knew. It felt safer to do that than to move on and take a risk. Once he saw the pattern, he understood why he had not been able to get clear on what he wanted to do with his life for more than six years. As a result, he became more willing, ready, and able to consider the inklings that had been begging for his attention for years.

Janelle noticed a theme of being a volunteer for groups that supported women's issues. She had spent her adult life being a certified public accountant, and had grown to hate the predictability of it, but did not see any other way to make a living. When asked about her interest in supporting the women's groups, she replied that she loved being around women that were doing so many different things. There were businesswomen, fund-raisers, executive directors of nonprofits, and they were all living full lives, many of them as single mothers like her. Up until this point, she had never realized that those women were all models of what could be possible for her and that she was spending time supporting them and not supporting her own hopes.

I saw further significance in her golden thread of support for women's issues. Her financial expertise would be a tremendous asset to many of these women's groups, since most of them are not-for-profit organizations. I could see her being a candidate for an executive directorship or other major role that would pay her as much as she made as a CPA. I saw the theme as her ticket out of misery. It had been there all along. Her Life Blueprint was there, only she had missed the clues. In fact, these threads were only the beginning of what ended up being a series of discoveries. You'll hear more about her story later.

A golden thread can also be an obvious lack of a certain element in someone's history. I was just working with a client who had been on a very straight, naturally progressive path in her professional pursuits. The sudden passing of her spouse two years prior had brought her to a point where she was reevaluating her life. She could not see any golden threads because she felt her personal history was "just her life" and because she was looking for a cluster of similar entries. However, I saw something lacking that built a theme. All of her accomplishments lacked "oomph." All her past jobs and careers were behind-the-scenes kinds of positions. Everything seemed very safe, and I pointed out that there was a lack of leadership in her history. She came back to our next appointment with some hesitance in her voice, but she said she had decided to step up to the plate into a leadership role in a community project she was working on. She was terrified to speak in public and to be perceived as unqualified, but she also knew that it was clearly the next step in her life to venture outside her comfort zone and lead.

Even if you can't interpret what your golden threads might mean, just concern yourself with finding them. It may help to let a few other people scan your history for clues as well.

Interrupted Dreams

Another clue is the *interrupted dream*. If there is a dream you had that got put on hold or pushed aside, or a dream that you keep procrastinating, you may have hit on another clue. If there is something that plagues you, but you cannot seem to bring it into your life no matter how much you think about it, it may be another significant clue worth examining. It may not mean that the immediate answer is to pick up where you left off, or to make it a priority in your life if it hasn't been before. However, it does hold value, and in the next chapter, we will analyze the interrupted dream further, but for now, simply identify if there is one.

Carla, the ex-champion gymnast, who you read about at the beginning of this chapter, is a great example of the interrupted dream. Sports was clearly not something she was going to go back to in the same way, but it was so ingrained in her that it needed to be included in some new way in order to honor her Life Blueprint and feel happy about her life again.

Corey had an interrupted dream, too. He had worked his way up the ladder over the years in the family furniture business. As the youngest of seven children, he worked alongside two other brothers in the business. Corey had never felt as though he had his family's support when he had talked of pursuing his dream to work in the music business someday. As a result, he went to work for his father, rationalizing that it was the sensible thing to do and would provide him the security and lifestyle that could include a family of his own one day.

When the family business went belly-up after several difficult years, Corey was faced with finding a job and figuring out what to do with his life. Scanning his personal history, he saw where his dream had been interrupted and why he had made the choices he had. It wasn't a comforting thought at first, because all he could focus on was the time he had wasted and the cost of trying to get back to the dream.

"Nothing is a waste," I said. (This is beginning to feel like a mantra!) "What part of your experience in your family's business can you apply to the music business?" I asked.

Corey thought about it and saw where his practice in maneuvering the politics of his family's business would be useful in breaking in to the politics of a whole different business. He also noticed his facility with the numbers of sales and warehousing, and how he could translate that to working for a record label. Although this put him no closer to making a transition to a new field, it did help him begin to think that his dream could be possible. Only then was he willing to try to make it a reality.

It took a lot of courage and determination and making money at odd jobs, but Corey did become a scout for a record label. He broke in after many initial rejections by going to clubs at his own expense and turning executives on to new talent. Once he had scored positively a few times, he was asked to come on board. He got back on track and did it!

Scan your history for where you may have gotten off track from a dream, and try to determine what its significance is today. Again, more help is coming your way in the next chapter.

Driving Motivators

A *driving motivator* is something, usually rooted in your childhood or young adulthood, that is driving your actions and decisions and that is probably not serving you very well anymore. It was a coping mechanism or survival skill you still use but that you have likely outgrown. It's probably a cause of your pain, but it's addictive and hard to quit. It is such a critical aspect of your makeup that you are literally blind to its trap.

Driving motivators are less about directing your next step, and more about halting a pattern that is keeping you from uncovering it. It's usually a pattern that keeps you unhappy, stressed, or stuck, but one that is so much a part of the fabric of your life that you may not even notice it is there. It will be more likely to be stopped, however, when you spot the source of it. If you did not spot it when we did the exercises about beliefs, it will most likely come up more clearly in this context.

Susan had a life story marred with workaholism and drive that most people would admire, but that's because they had no idea what her motivation was. When Susan was 17 years old, she was on track to a college scholarship for her outstanding talent on the baseball field. Her first sexual encounter with her longtime, steady boyfriend resulted in a pregnancy that cut her college and baseball plans short. She had declared at 17 that she would not become a statistic and that she would beat the odds of unwed teenage mothers, which she has many times over. She had a beautiful child, married the father two years later, and is still happily married to him. However, she has worked three times as hard as anyone in her job, her marriage, her mothering, and everything she touches—to prove to her family, and whoever else may know her, that she is a worthy person.

It wasn't until she wrote her personal history that she saw the driving motivator that was making her miserable now. She saw that she had a choice between continuing to be driven by the past and deciding to behave differently today. To suddenly discover that being a workaholic is optional was incredibly freeing for Susan. She had so many choices as to what direction her life could take once the pattern was identified and the ball and chain were off.

Tom had a very different driving motivator. He was known by everyone as the guy who'd give you the shirt off his back or give away his last dime—admirable qualities, if it really made him happy to do so. But Tom did not operate from a mind-set of having found his place in life as a perpetual giver; he was more accurately driven by guilt. He grew up in an environment where money did not flow freely, and his parents always cried poor. He began, at a very early age, to feel guilty if he ever had anything desirable at all—money, a new toy, candy that no one else had. He learned that the pain of his guilt could be assuaged by giving away what he had. If what he did have made him feel guilty, he felt better when he gave it away. It's not that it made him feel *good* to give it away; it just made him feel *better*.

This pattern followed him into adulthood, and he gave away his ideas, didn't accept credit where credit was due, and led a bit of a substandard life because he never kept his money or bothered with managing his belongings. He also was the first to help anyone in trouble, which often cost him money, time, and a lot of peace of mind, as he often tried to help people who really were not ready to change. When his job in the tech industry dried up, he was truly at a loss as to what he would do with his life.

By the time Tom got to me, he was searching for what was next. When he wrote his personal history and saw guilt as his driving motivator, he was stunned. He reported feeling dumbfounded for a couple weeks, but when he gripped it fully, he agreed that he could choose to act differently. It was not easy, because the opposite had been automatic for so long, but he did feel very encouraged that his life could change just by making this discovery. It turned out that he was still very attracted to giving and helping professions, but realizing that he could be motivated by something positive made the difference in his ultimate success. He eventually retrained and made his way into nursing.

In one of my recent seminars, a man shared that up until the point he was currently at in his life, everything he had done or accomplished was because he "should" do it. He had just come to realize that his whole life was based on what he "should" do and that it basically was dictated by something other than his truest self and his truest desires. It was a sobering admission, but one that can be useful here for you to see how we get off track from our Life Blueprint.

If you find that you have a driving motivator that serves you up more trouble than good, take a moment to name it and to realize that you get to choose again. If you are being driven by something you would rather not be driven by, realize that you can do it differently. Realize the source, ask yourself what was significant about that place where you broke off contact with your self, and then immediately start changing the lens you see life through. It starts one thought at a time, one choice at a time. For example, if you had unexpectedly found out that you have type 1 diabetes, you would have to watch your sugar intake and choose your foods differently. Similarly, if you have a propensity for being driven by a negative motivator, watch yourself like a hawk and stop yourself before you act from there. You have another choice. Choose right, and recognize that this driving motivator is keeping you off your Life Blueprint.

What You Are Good At Isn't Always "It"

After reviewing your history and being aware of the significant themes, you may be surprised to discover that what you are very good at (and probably have been good at for a very long time) has not been one of your benchmarks in this process. Many people mistakenly have adopted the tenet that if you are good at something, it is a clue as to what you need to be doing with your life. But that is not necessarily true. It may remain a part of what makes you successful, but it may not be "it." It may have been "it," but it is no longer "it" if you are no longer happy doing it. It was simply a well-developed muscle, the strength of which will still serve you, but it does not need to be taxed any longer. If you have been sticking with something for this reason, please know that you are now free! Being good at something is *not* the surefire sign that it's your destiny.

Barry was in exactly this situation. He was a computer genius and had been a programmer for many years after getting his degree at the Massachusetts Institute of Technology (MIT). He was great with computers, had a deep respect for them, and was grateful for the living he made working with them. However, he had outgrown the challenge, and there was no "next step" that was attractive or immediately obvious to him. He was at a loss as to what else he would do, because there was no other obvious thing that he was equally good at.

Once he allowed himself to look at things he was not good at (yet), he saw that he loved business (he also had a Harvard MBA) and could use his knowledge of technology to relate to other people in the technology fields. He fell on the coaching profession in an industry magazine, and saw how his interests in business and technology could hook up. He could coach people who work in technology companies on the business side of the biz while helping the individuals grow. He found "it" once he let go of the notion that what he was good at was his only available option for change.

The thought that you can actually outgrow a situation or skill might be tough to swallow, but it's true. Once it becomes dull, boring, or a chore, either it's time for a bigger challenge in the same area of concentration or it's time to move on. You know it's time to move on if all your efforts to challenge yourself or get reconnected to the skill go unanswered by satisfaction, fulfillment, and excitement. If your answer is just to try harder, discipline yourself more, or push yourself, you are barking up the wrong tree. No matter how hard you try, if you do not have a strong connection to your skill or like who you get to be by doing it, it is time to evolve and move on to the next thing. And even though we are excavating for "it," remember, "it" will change over time as you do, and that's a good thing.

Past–Promise Phenomenon

Other times, things you were good at in the past may be the connection to getting back on track with your Life Blueprint in the present. What is fascinating to me is the wisdom embedded in your life. You must go back to where you left off being your genuine, unadulterated self to pick up the momentum that is needed to break through to clarity and new direction. Whether you found that place through the lens of Golden Threads, Interrupted Dreams, or Driving Motivators does not matter. What does matter is that you take the time to reconnect with yourself as you were at the moment in time when you were caused to go down a path that diverged from joy.

As I said before, for many people, that place is determined by an activity, interest, or strength that dates back to a point in childhood or young adulthood. The dilemma is that it is not always clear how to bring that past promise into today. Take Carla, the gymnast. She was not going to start doing back handsprings at 32 years old, nor was Jon, the magician, going to set up shop and do kids' birthday parties again. The correlation is not meant to be that literal. What does need to happen, however, is that the past-promise, that activity that held so much potential happiness for you, needs to be revisited. Sometimes that can mean literally doing it again, not as a career or direction, but as a visit that brings you back to center and to yourself. This reconnection often causes a breakthrough. That is your payoff.

Maria grew up in East LA in a deeply Latino community. She did not have much luxury, but life was good. Maria had access to a piano and had shown great promise at an early age. An opportunity to study with a teacher whose students often went on to Juilliard came her way. Even as her talent was nurtured and her abilities were strengthened, "real" life took hold, and Maria had to take responsibility for her siblings and give up her study of the piano. After raising her brothers and sisters, followed by her own kids and family, the piano was a long-buried treasure in her life story. However, while working with her coach, Pam Richarde — my esteemed partner in the Life Blueprint Institute — she discovered the piano again.

While looking at Maria's life story, Pam and I both agreed that the answers to her future were in the past's promise of the piano. Pam walked Maria into a practice room at Berkley College and left her to get reacquainted with the instrument. It wasn't as easy for Maria as we had hoped to face this part of her past. She showed some resistance to recommitting to music, but she wrote to Pam soon after to tell her of a significant reminder she received.

It turned out that Maria was at a party where there was a palm reader doing readings for the guests. When it came to Maria's turn, the reader said that Maria had been involved with music and that she had to get back to her music now. Maria wrote Pam the next day to ask if there was a conspiracy going on. Whether you believe in palm readers or not, you have to admit that was quite the "coincidence." Maria could not ignore the advice now that it was coming to her through another means. Each time she played, she got more clarity about what she needed to do to take care of herself in her life. It started with setting boundaries with some of her children who were not respectful of her. The process was slow, but it was as if she gained strength and clarity with each practice session. We have big hopes for Maria.

Jim was a golf pro when he was in his 20s, but had been in business full time for fifteen years when I met him. He had been struggling to get a new business venture off the ground. He had plenty of capital, but was burning through it at a rapid rate, and he was unsure about what his next steps should be. Should he get out while he still could? Would it behoove him to keep raising capital? What possibilities did he have at hand to solve his problem?

With no answers coming, I sent Jim back to his past-promise to find the answer. He had been away from his golf game for a long time because of the stress and distraction of his business. But given the permission and hope of a solution, he worked on his game almost daily until he started to see his way to clarity. His solution for his business was to create a merger with another company, but it was only through his connection to his past-promise that he saw it. He got the "ah-ha" as he studied himself and his swing. The word "merge" kept coming into his head. He thought it was about the game, until he realized it was about his business, too.

I can attest to the phenomenon myself. I willingly gave up singing along with my acting career, and moved on to other things, obviously. I sang for fun with a local choir in my community until my first child was born, followed by my first book and a new life of travel and entrepreneurship. I did not even really miss singing in public, and would feel plenty fulfilled by a good sing-along to a Barbra Streisand CD while driving alone in the car. A couple of years ago, however, while on tour with my second book, I felt like something was missing from my presentations. I felt my talks never ended with the oomph I wanted them to. I was at a loss as to what to do until I spent some time reviewing the places where I had shown promise in the past. Singing was an obvious one.

The first time I ended a talk with a song was in Toronto, and as I write this, I can still vividly feel the lump in my throat that choked me to tears while I eeked out my first public singing in a decade. The crowd cried with me and went mad with applause when it was over. I don't cry anymore when I do it, and I only include a song if the mood seems right, but that first try gave me the breakthrough I was looking for and the oomph my talks needed. Once again, the past-promise held the key to the other side.

Where did you show promise in the past? How could it help you get in touch with your Life Blueprint and future path? I hope you'll take the time to explore this concept, in addition to the other directions included here for using your life story to open up possibilities moving forward.

Funneling Regrets

Suddenly recognizing that you've been hanging out there in some career or life choice that has nothing to do with who you really are can cause a very panicked feeling. It's like building your dream house, only to find out that you are allergic to the wood you made it out of. It is very hard to extricate yourself from the life you may have already created once you realize it does not match who you really are. Often, this can begin the regret roller coaster—the sinking feeling that you are trapped, that you made your bed and now have to lie in it, forever. *Not true.*

Although you may not see your immediate way out, and may not even know what else you would replace your current life with, there is a transitional point that you can now set into motion. It is exactly why I have asked you to get used to looking at yourself in terms of *who* you get to be vs. *what* you used to do. The first step out of anything is to start being fully *who* you are, even under the pressure, disdain, or misery of your current situation or job. It requires no job search or life planning, which makes it the most available and immediate option you have. You've got nothing to lose by trying to right a situation that is so wrong. If this technique fails, you will have all the confirmation you need that it is time do something about your situation anyway!

Take the next step; correct what doesn't work. And please don't tell me you can't, or that your current situation does not allow you to. No one and nothing *allows* you to do or not do something. In the end, it is *you* who is holding yourself back. Telling the truth about who you are and what you want will get the ball rolling. As this next story will attest, you've got nothing to lose.

Patti, who works in hospital administration, had just finished telling me how horrible her work environment was and how it did not allow her to be herself. She told me that she was a fun person and that her workplace did not allow any of that to come through. She felt reasonably certain that her only option was to leave this environment, although the hospital was ready to promote her and get her on the VP track. She did not want the opportunity because it felt, in her words, "like a life sentence."

I had no doubt that Patti was telling the truth, and I know that negative places can squelch anyone's spirit, but there was one thing she had not tried that would give her a definitive answer whether it was time to stay or move on. That thing was being herself. Instead of altering herself to match her environment, I challenged her to be her fun self at work—just fully, totally be herself. She was surprised at the simplicity of the idea, and we both agreed that one cannot get fired for being happy and maybe even silly at work, so she agreed to give it a try.

Now, this will sound too good to be true, but it is 100 percent true! When Patti spent a week letting her hair down at work, the conversation about getting on the VP track came due. To her own surprise, in the meeting with her boss, she spoke up about what she needed to get out of the job, and her most significant demand was that the job be fun! Her boss spent the rest of their time together trying to convince her that the job would be fun, should she choose to take it. Patti said it felt like a complete turnaround. One shift in her perception, and the whole situation changed. That is the power of telling the truth about who you are and what you want: You often get it!

Patti proceeded cautiously, but now she knew she had more influence over the situation than she had previously thought.

> ### Exercise: *Who Are You?*

Take one more look at your personal history and its bullet points. In the margins, write down *who* you were, *who* you got to be, or *who* you are during each of the most significant themes or achievements. For example, if the passing of a relative or parent colored your life, write down *who* you were because of it. You might write: "A time of great sadness, but I was the strong one the family relied on to get through." Or upon receiving that high-school award, record *who* you got to be. Maybe you got to be someone who felt destined to do something great.

If the "who" deals with something negative, like a certain career ending, and you felt like someone who failed or missed an opportunity, write that down as well. You will use this information in the next chapter.

Discomfort Equals Growth

This chapter may have shot your blood pressure up a few notches. This point in the process is where I usually start to hear such comments as: "This is scary" or "This is getting serious now; I really have to do something about my complaining" or "This is exciting, but I feel light-headed." Don't worry. We are pushing the parameters of your comfort zone. It is appropriate and common to be feeling a little uncomfortable at this point. And I'll tell you what I tell my clients: discomfort = growth.

When you are being stretched beyond your comfort zone, you are being asked to grow. You have to take risks and be willing to be wrong. You are being asked to step into the unknown, and by now I hope you can see that it is necessary if you are serious about changing your life.

I made the observation that discomfort equals growth when my oldest son was only a few months old. I had started to notice that any sleepless or disrupted nights he had were immediately followed by a growth spurt. A sleepless night might unveil a new tooth or reveal that the pajamas I put on him the night before did not fit in the morning.

Growth is uncomfortable. If it wasn't, we'd be changing ourselves and our life at every whim. We humans don't like to be uncomfortable, but perhaps if we can keep it in perspective and understand that discomfort means that change is under way, it might help us remain calm. Kids have growing pains. So do adults. It will be worth it. Hang in there.

▶ Questions to Ponder

What surprised me that I did not remember about my personal history?

What golden threads, interrupted dreams, or driving motivators did I find?

What, if anything, can be of service to you now from a past-promise or strength?

What have I learned about myself as a result of this chapter?

What speaks to me at this point as confirmation of possible future directions?

Who did I get to be in the past that I liked? Who was I that I was not happy with?

Your Purpose in Life Is Right Under Your Nose

Just when I discovered the meaning of life,
it changed.

—GEORGE CARLIN

The purpose of life is a life of purpose.

—ROBERT BYRNE

I've already explained that the one overriding theme to my work over the last few years has been that my clients have been on a quest for more meaning in their life. Whether it is through meaningful work or just getting a better handle on creating meaning in their relationships and casual interactions in life, the people I've been working with have been exploring what "meaning" means to them. Everyone's definition of meaning will be different, but this chapter will reveal that what is meaningful lies with you and no one else. Here, you will learn how to discover what is meaningful to you—a step that is crucial to feeling happy with your life.

The struggle to feel as though our lives have meaning has always been part of our existential angst as human beings, but now you will begin to answer this internal query and put that answer into action. Meaning is the ticket to the future that you are longing to create. In essence, meaning is what ties life together so it makes sense. It's that something that gets you out of bed in the morning and gives direction to your day and your life.

The biggest shift you will need to make in this 90-day process is an evolutionary step in your personal development. It's the kind of life-changing step I believe millions of people have been drawn to make in the last few years. You will shift from the singular focus of you and your goals to the more global reach of how your life impacts the world for the better. It does not mean we are all becoming angelic, altruistic souls; it means our souls are asking us to adopt a larger vision of who we are.

This is the undercurrent to our longings and inquiries about life. We want to know that we matter and that we can make a difference. We would like to know how we fit into the whole. But above all, we want peace of mind. We want to feel better, we want to feel good. The answer is finding our sense of purpose. *Meaning.*

My guess is that the most surprising part of what you are about to discover is that meaning and purpose are right under your nose. Meaning is not something you invent, or force, or manipulate to sound good. It is something you come to recognize. It will simply require a refocusing of something that is already there. It's like an Escher print—the image looks like one thing, but when you focus on it another way, it's a different picture entirely. Once you see the new picture, your eyes cannot help but focus there. Similarly, once you bring your new purpose to the surface, it will be ingrained as a permanent part of the landscape. Best of all, it will not require a tremendous turnaround or effort to start living from that place.

Finding a sense of purpose is especially helpful in redirecting your work life, but that's not necessarily the only place where it will come in handy. Some of you might discover that finding meaningful work may not be as important to you as you thought, as long as your work allows you the time and freedom to pursue what is most meaningful to you. Many people find a sense of peace in recognizing their job as the financial support of a life that is productive and purposeful.

If you are going through this process to redirect your life after divorce or some other kind of transition or loss, you will also benefit from pointing your life to something bigger than the problems you are faced with at the moment. Connecting with a sense of purpose elevates your growth, and its discovery often accelerates the progress of your healing and transition.

I now offer you three access points that have worked to unearth a clear purpose for people I have worked with: who you are to others, what your dreams really mean, and what people reflect upon you. One of these three can work to open up this exploration for you, so don't be concerned if you try one and it doesn't work. I suggest trying all three seeing if you see any similarities in your answers. However, it may be that only one successfully accesses an answer about purpose while the others do not.

Who You Are to Others

As we ended the last chapter, you took stock of *who* you were in those significant moments in your personal history. Now we will take stock of who you are to those around you as a step toward finding meaning and purpose in your life.

No one has a purpose alone in a vacuum. What you are meant to do with your life, and how you impact your world, will always be about you affecting other people. As Winston Churchill once said, "We make a living by what we get; we make a life by what we give." Here is the opportunity to see how you make a difference every day—probably in ways you did not even imagine. Why do you think we watch *It's a Wonderful Life* every Christmas season, even though we know the story inside and out? This wonderful film reminds us that our existence has a ripple effect—that we get to decide what we leave in our wake. Recognizing how you impact other people becomes crucial to moving your life in a more satisfying direction.

> ### Exercise: *Who You Are to Others*

Think of all the people in your life: family, friends, co-workers, neighbors, and others in your community or environment. Take pen to paper and write down what each of those people tends to come to you for. How do they use you? What do they seem to call on you for? What effect do you seem to have on them? What are they naturally attracted to you for? Use the following example for guidance.

Family: come to me for source of strength

Neighbors: come to me for examples of how to do things

Coworkers: come to me to figure out how to get things done

Friends: come to me to work through problems
   step-by-step

Community: comes to me to ask me to volunteer for
   projects, because they know I will get them done

When you have done this, look for the theme, or similarity, among the different categories and draw a conclusion about who you naturally are to other people. Massage your answer to reveal the purest form of how you touch other people. There may be a few layers of interpretation before it crystallizes to the point where it resonates with you as someone you enjoy getting to be. Refine it until it is meaningful for you.

Example of a Conclusion

Version 1: Who I am to others is someone who gets things
   done.
Version 2: Who I am is a teacher, a guide, a how-to manual.
Version 3: Who I am is someone who empowers others to
   be self-fulfilled.

The natural, built-in use that you provide to the world is part of your Life Blueprint. It has always been there. You can probably trace it very far back in your life—sometimes as far as childhood, but most of the time, from late adolescence or young adulthood on.

Maria had always recognized that people came to her for advice and guidance. She was working as an administrative assistant when she came to explore what was next for her life. In her administrative role, she supported others in her office, and that was meaningful to her, but she was bored and unchallenged, and she knew there had to be more.

Maria's creativity started to flow after she got confirmation that something that always occurred naturally in her life (giving advice and guidance) could actually be what she was built to do. For the first time in a long time, she had ideas about what else she could do for a living because this confirmation allowed her to live with a newly rediscovered sense of purpose.

You will put some form to your discoveries a bit later, as Maria came to do. She found she could get enthusiastic about expressing her sense of purpose—that is, being a source of advice and guidance—through such careers as lawyer, working with children or teenagers, counselor, or manager of a resort property. She knew retraining would be required, but having a clear sense of her purpose gave her comfort and motivation to get on a new path.

Dysfunctional "Who"

But sometimes who you are isn't necessarily who you are meant to be. One of my clients, Bettie, was doing this exploration and saw that she was the perpetual volunteer, the worker bee, the one to go to in a pinch, or the one who would do anything for anybody. She hated to see those words staring back at her on the page. She sounded so discouraged as she asked me if that was who she was meant to be in this life. After all, it was there, it was undeniable, and it must have been part of her Life Blueprint—or so she thought.

"No, Bettie, this is not your purpose," I said.

"But how do you know?" she answered.

"It carries no joy. It's causing you pain. It stems from a wound, not a gift," I said. "It's what you are meant to get over, so your true purpose can come through."

When you have been operating from a place that needs to be healed (preferably identified and worked through in therapy), you are wrestling with a life lesson, not necessarily your purpose. Nonetheless, if you can shift the same activities (like Bettie's penchant for serving others) to a place of joy and wholeness, then it may very well be part of the blueprint you are meant to pursue. If Bettie really felt connected to what she was doing, if she felt her small pieces added up to a whole that she believed in and that benefited others, she would be on track, and it would be worth it to stay on course. But it wasn't, and it needed to be changed.

Bettie's example shows us a common issue that you might find in this exploration. Oftentimes, a person's greatest gift can be his or her greatest burden or flaw. If something that comes naturally to you also squeezes the joy out of your life, it obviously needs to be reexamined. Some of the negative driving motivators we discussed in the last chapter could be at work, so look for your motivation, or the original source of you using this gift in a way that is burdening you. What motivates you to keep doing what you are doing?

Guilt is often a driving force. Is your talent something you or your family spent a lot of money educating you on? Is it something that you are afraid will cost you in some other way if you stop doing it? Do you feel that your gift is the reason you have people in your life, and that if you did not use it, the people would go away? Are you afraid that if you stopped living this gift, you would not know what to do with yourself?

So many times, a strength, gift, or talent has gotten misdirected. That doesn't mean you have to exclude it from your life, it just needs to be directed in a way that brings you energy instead of it exhausting you. Who you are to others is how you will be of service to the world, but you are also allowed to gauge how often you expend energy on it and how much you give. If you don't, and it turns into dysfunction, the gift will be gone. It's like chocolate: A little bit is a treat; a boxful is a stomachache. Go easy, use your gifts correctly, and they will bring you joy.

Separating the Yolk from the Whites

We just keep excavating to bring out the core of you, don't we? Well, here, we will go even further to uncover your unique purpose by giving you a second way to explore it. We need to separate the yolk from the whites, as I like to say. What I mean is that hidden in some of your life decisions is a more meaningful purpose and direction for your talents than you may have realized. Logical, practical decisions may have separated you from that golden center, or life may have gotten in the way. However, we want to reclaim that now so we can define your next steps.

In Chapter Two, we talked about mourning loss even if it was the result of positive change. We talked about letting go of the package and moving the transferable net gain of your experiences forward. To separate the yolk from the whites, we will look to the "package" again, but this time the package will be your dreams — perhaps that dream you left on the side of the road that you rediscovered when you did your personal history, or maybe a dream that you are hoping to bring into reality now. In any case, we are going to dissect your dream to see if we can find the richness that will point you in a new direction.

When we have a dream or a vision for ourselves, we create a package for it and pursue that package or we mourn the lack of its presence in our lives. But the package can be misleading. Your dream may be unrequited if you only focus on the package. (Not all of us have been as fortunate as Tiger Woods, who dreamed of being the best in his field, executed it, and became it.) When we believe that the form our dreams take is what will bring us happiness, we lose sight of how our dreams are most valuable to us. The part of the dream that holds the clues is not in the whites, but in the yolk. The yolk is the golden center that lies within the package. It is the part of the dream that reveals *who* you are meant to be vs. *what* you are meant to do.

The package is the what; what's inside the package is the who—*who* you get to be because of the dream. That is the gold, the part that you have available to you immediately. It is the essence of the dream (the essence of you) that is the valuable information, not the package you have visualized to express yourself.

The mistake that we make is that we focus on the package, and, for most of us, the package is rigid. Being a broadcaster, a businessperson, a world traveler, a parent, or whatever your dream is does not leave room for negotiation. You either become that thing or you don't. But when you focus on the essence of the dream, you are dealing with something malleable. You are dealing with *who* you get to be by doing it. It can fit in many other packages and come in many other forms. It can move. A rigid dream cannot. Thus it is not the dream's form you necessarily want as much as what you think the dream offers.

I remember a woman sitting in the front row of one of my talks. She sprung up in her seat upon hearing me talk about the essence of the dream. I could tell that something had just become possible for her, so I asked her to share it with the audience. She explained how she had been very frustrated by her dream of being a television newscaster. She had been trying desperately to break in, with little or no luck. She saw that that was the rigid package and left only two options: being a newscaster or not be-ing a newscaster.

The shift that occurred for her was that in examining the essence of her dream, she saw that what she really wanted from being a newscaster was to be a source of information that could affect people's lives for the better. She saw that she could do that in so many other ways. She already was a writer, and that work came to her easily, so she saw that she could take bigger strides there and stop suffering over the newscaster business. By revolv-ing her life around her purpose instead of the package she had chosen, she had so many more options. You could see the relief and excitement on her face. That is what I want for you.

> ### Exercise: *The Essence of the Dream*

Bring forth the burning dream or desire you have within you now, or one that you had to abandon a long time ago (even if you have no desire to do it now). Alternatively, you might write down all the things you have dreamed of doing at one time or another and look for what they have in common.

Take pen to paper and ask yourself: What would be (or would have been) possible if I became successful at my dream(s)?

Answer, and pay specific attention to how you would impact other people and the world if you were to succeed at the package you have chosen. What would be possible for people or the world if you succeeded at your dream?

Your answer will yield the yolk, the essence that the

dream really represents—the *who* you are built to be. We will worry about *what* package can make you a living later.

Here are some samples:

Package	Essence
Writer	challenges the mind
Vice president of a company	can affect change
Actor	impacts people's lives
Business owner	improves women's lives

Note: The essence you come up with for the same packages may be different, these are only examples of possibilities.

Some people are lucky enough to have reached many of their dreams. Jon, for example, hadn't had any deficit of dreams in his life. In fact, he'd had many. So he decided to look at all the wishes he had had over the course of his life to see what they had in common.

When Jon was a young boy, he dreamed of being a magician. As time went on, he outgrew that notion and went off to college to study architecture and design. He spent many years as a branding expert at advertising agencies, and then went freelance with his design work shortly before I met him.

In addition to being a magician, he had, over the course of his life, become an architect, industrial designer, inventor, consultant, and outdoor gear designer, and he dabbled in geology and was an outdoor adventure guide. When he first searched this list for the common theme, he was stumped, but suddenly it dawned on him. All his desires nurtured a sense of wonder in him and others. All the dreams were an attempt to define, create, express, and communicate a sense of wonder. Suddenly, it made sense to him why he had made some of the choices he did and what choices he had to make in the present. He realized that he wanted to have an impact on other people by getting them in touch with their sense of wonder. His central purpose became crystal clear to him, and so many things made sense as a result. His purpose was to work with people to experience a sense of wonder from the natural world. Jon's hobby was outdoor adventure and nature exploration. In defining his purpose, he could see that his hobby was meant to be a bigger part of his life. He admitted that his ultimate dream at that point in his life was to become the owner of an outdoor adventure company, or to be involved with one in some way. He began to look at how his other experience could marry with outdoor adventure to move him on to his next step.

At first, Jon had trouble thinking of a dream to use in the exercise, because he had accomplished so many of his dreams in his life. On the other hand, there may be some of you who might say you've never had a dream. It happens.

Anyone who has to work extremely hard to get by or who had an emotionally disruptive childhood, or one that required them to work or mature from innocent play sooner than normal, might find that they don't feel wired for dreaming or visioning. Even if you are just naturally more of a doer kind of person, your visioning or dreaming muscles may be a little weak.

It's OK if you haven't found your dream. If you are not working from something you wanted to do or be, or an idea of where you saw yourself in the future, you can still work the dream exercise. If you want to stop doing something or want out of your current situation, that is a dream in itself. Let's say you would like to stop being a CPA. You may not have any idea what could replace your current role, but you are clear that you want out. In the exercise, you would use the same question: What would be possible (for others and the world) if I was no longer a CPA? What would I be free to express or do? It's a lofty question, I know, but think about it. If you were free from something that clips your wings, then it would be possible to more fully be yourself. To feel and be happier is a significant contribution to the world around you. The world would be a nicer place if everyone felt that way. So, is your life purpose to be free to feel happier? Yes, for now it is. As you do this for yourself, you'll be an example for other people as well. In time your sense of purpose will evolve into something different.

Don't be discouraged if you haven't found your vision or dream. It just means it is time to take care of yourself and get your life in order. You can expect your wiring for dreaming to kick in as you get things in order.

For those of you who did find your purpose, please do not be concerned if your purpose does not reflect some potentially huge or altruistic impact. (Very few of us are meant to be the next Gandhi!) And if you are one of the people who has yet to gain clarity on some sense of purpose, the next access point should help.

People Are Your Mirror

We've addressed the things for which people rely on you, and the meaning of the dreams you've had or not had. Now we will look at a third place where you may find your sense of purpose. It lies in how people have reflected on your talents and strengths.

Is there a theme to what people have always said you should do or be? Have they always said you should be a cop, a lawyer, a model, a CEO, or some other specific role? We are looking here for something that has come up over and over again—maybe not for your entire life, although that is possible. It could be something that has come up recently. Nonetheless, it's some kind of ongoing message that those around you have continually delivered to you.

If there is a theme, bring it into the mix of this discussion. It does not necessarily mean that you are meant to run off and do that very thing, but it may hold some clues for us in your quest for direction. As we did with your dream, we need to extract the yolk from the egg. The significance of what people have reflected about you is not the package itself (the *what*) but the *who* that might accompany it. Which qualities are they picking up about you? That is what we want to focus on.

> ### Exercise: *What Do People Say?*

Write down what people have always said you "should" be. Drawing from the other two exercises in this chapter, try to come up with the *who* that corresponds to the *what*. For example, let's say people have always said you should be a poet because you are great with words. Whether you actually write poetry or not is not the point. Rather, look at what that signifies in terms of who a poet is in the world. You might say poets are people who move people to think, feel, or act by using words. Discard the package of "poet" and hold on to the part about being someone who moves people to think, feel, or act by using words. This part may be our clue for a future direction.

If you are not sure if people have said such things about you, it's OK to sit down with a few trusted people and ask what they see in you or what they see you doing in the future.

Take a moment to record what you have learned.

Having people bestow their opinion upon you about what you should do with your life can hold significant clues. Martin was always being told how funny he was and that he should become a stand-up comic. Naturally, he was very flattered whenever he heard this, and even toyed with the notion of pursuing stand-up comedy. However, at a closer glance, Martin saw that he really had no interest in living the lifestyle that being a comic would require. He had a wife and a daughter, and he did not want to struggle.

Martin was, however, at a crossroads in his life. He had been a technical writer for many years and was growing bored and weary but really did not know what else he could do. When he read one of my books and came across the notion of revolving his life around a central purpose, he wrote to tell me what he discovered. He found that when people said he should be a comic, they were showing him the impact he had on people. He made them laugh. He made them look at things in a different way. In recognizing this, he swelled with a sense of pride and realized he had found his purpose. (See, it is not rocket science to discover it, and it *is* right under your nose!)

Martin looked at how else he could package his humor, and he knew that he already had what he needed. He began writing humorous editorial pieces commenting on the trivial things in life while continuing to work at technical writing. Slowly, he began to get his new pieces into newspapers. Now he intends to cross over completely from technical writing to humor, and he is even looking into what it would take to write for television. He was able to start moving his life forward once he recognized his purpose and the message that others were reflecting to him.

One barrier to accepting what others see in you as an indication of purpose is having a self-image that is completely opposite to what others see. One woman told me that everyone around her tells her that she is a positive source of encouragement and always sees what's good. However, on the inside, she only sees flaws and was surprised to hear how others saw her. Another woman was surprised that other people expressed how she makes them feel at ease and yet, inside, she thinks she is not flexible at all and that she is rigid and tense.

We are often harder on ourselves than we are on other people. If you get feedback that opposes your self-assessment, don't discard it. Take a moment to absorb the message in it. Maybe your self-assessment is off. Maybe it's time to treat yourself the way you treat other people. This process of self-discovery will help open up your creativity and success.

What Has Your Life Been About?

The three access points that we just covered usually succeed in revealing your core essence, but in a few, rare cases there has been one more exploration needed to finish the job. That inquiry is this simple question: "What has your life been about?"

If you scanned your life from even a wider perspective than you used in doing your life story, and tried to say what your life represented as a whole, what would it be? I realize that is not an easy question, but sometimes your interpretation of your life's theme can indicate which personal resources you are now meant to turn into a well of wisdom to help others.

Once, for example, I was working with a woman at one of the *Now What?* seminars to sharpen her articulation of her purpose. She was struggling with the task, and I would not relent in insisting that she be able to articulate it in a way that resonated as being truthful and genuine. (Talking about one's "purpose" can get very airy-fairy and highfalutin very quickly.) I wanted her to be able to state something that did not sound like a baloney, pat statement that would just end up being more confusing than useful to her. As she grew more frustrated with herself, and me, I asked her: "What has your life been about?" In frustration, she replied: "Overcoming obstacles!"

"Do you feel qualified to help other people overcome obstacles?" I asked.

"Yes!" she retorted emphatically.

"Congratulations. You've found your purpose."

What happened in that moment for that woman (and what may be available to you) is that a critical turning point occurred in her realization and understanding of her purpose. It was now possible for her to give up the identification of herself as someone who had a difficult life or who was suffering unfairly, and to take on the wisdom that life had given her as something useful that had meaning. She went from being a helpless bystander in her own circumstances to someone who was empowered to be a source of strength for other people. This is so important, because it is a critical spiritual milestone for any person to stop living their life as a happenstance and start using their life a chosen purpose. Can you see how this makes life much more meaningful? Can you see how it can give someone a tremendous focus or cornerstone? Can you see how possibilities can flow from this

turning point, instead of being stuck on the other side and being
blocked?

> ### Exercise: *What Has Your Life Been About?*

Look over your life story from the last chapter again. Is
there anything that jumps out as an overriding theme?
This time, we are not looking for golden threads but for
themes that represent an arc of obstacles or life lessons, or
an arc of emotion or tests. For example, has your life been
about sacrifice, finding your own way, beating the odds, or
fighting prejudice and cultural limits? Has it been about
charity, caretaking, advocacy, or ritual? Perceived positive
or negatives, either one, could be useful here.

Write down the possibilities that occur to you and see
how they fit into the rest of what you have learned about
meaning and purpose. Declare a purpose.

Eureka!

How do you know you've found it? How do you know if you've
uncovered a sense of purpose that can serve you as you move forward? I'll tell you. There are two simple criteria. One is that your
purpose is something that requires no retraining. You are instantly qualified to perform it, because it has been part of you all
along. Granted, if you were to make a career of it, you may need
some formal training or a certificate or license, but for the most
part, it is something you can do immediately in some form.

The second criterion, which we touched on briefly, is that
your purpose is something that impacts other people. It is an an-

swer to how you serve the whole. Even if you think it's small, it doesn't matter. Not everyone's purpose is meant to be grand. If it impacts other people in a positive way, it is a purpose. It is the essence of you, and it must move forward with you as you name your next step.

You will immediately feel differently about your life and your situation when you start living from a sense of purpose every day. All you need to do is turn up the volume on your purpose. It was there all along; you just were not focusing on it. You were focusing on *what* you were doing and *what* you wanted, not on *who* you were being. So, if you turn up the volume on the *who*, you will start to move your life in a new direction immediately, even if you haven't named what "it" is.

This is why I often call your purpose your "lucrative" purpose. It can bring you money and opportunity but, more important, it is lucrative in how it greases the wheel, so to speak, helping you to get more out of your life: more enjoyment, more ease, more possibility.

Something else you may have noticed here, especially if you are one of those over-achiever, perfectionist folks (takes one to know one, but I am recovering, thanks!): living from a sense of purpose is a tremendous relief. It takes a lot of the pressure to achieve off you. In fact, it gives you many more opportunities to feel you have achieved, because it is not necessarily goal-oriented. It does not require many steps to declare success. You can be successful at your purpose in small, instant ways. This, in turn, does allow some of the bigger goals to come more quickly and with less effort, because the focus is not on what is missing. The focus is not on how far you still have to go. The focus is on something immediately achievable that then breeds more success. What a relief, huh?

It may also invite you to recognize that ambition may have been your biggest obstacle to peace. It is OK to be ambitious, unless it causes you great pain and angst. See, when you are ambitious, but fueled by purpose instead of fueled by the need to prove something (such as your own worthiness), it becomes OK to love your life even if you are not yet at the pinnacle of your vision. It becomes easier to take risks. If your consolation prize is that your life stays the same, and that life feels good, then going for something outrageous becomes a fun game. What do you have to lose if you have not put your happiness or self-worth at stake? This is such an easier place to achieve from. You get to be a winner every day. After all, why suffer when you can set yourself up to win?

Who You'd Like to Be

We are one step away from starting to name possible future directions for you, but before we do, we are going to plunge one step deeper. We are cementing your orientation around *who* you are before we try to find *what* you might do next. You spent this chapter getting a hold on a sense of purpose and seeing that it's about the essence of who you are as a person—nothing less, nothing more. What I'd like to know now is who you'd like to be as you move forward, and what kind of person you'd like to be in the new life that you are creating.

> ### Exercise: *Who Would You Like to Be?*

Jot down a list of who's. Who would you like to become as you move forward? What kind of person would you like to be? For example:

I want to be someone who is cheerful.

I want to be someone who can take criticism but not take it personally.

I want to be someone who is kinder to myself and everyone around me.

I want to be someone who is encouraging to everyone around me.

Putting your list of *who*'s first makes for an easier way to live. Chevon came to one of my seminars and explained what changed in her life when she adopted putting *who* she wanted to be ahead of *what* she wanted to succeed at. She was living in New York to pursue her dream of being a singer. She had had her share of disappointments and caught herself just short of quitting when she realized she could take a different approach to her life and her career. She decided to live her life according to the criteria of *who* she wanted to be. Being kind, helpful to people, sunny in her disposition, and full of life became the horse to her cart, so to speak.

She told us that her luck started changing as soon as she put *who* she wanted to be at the forefront. She had never thought of pursuing musical theatre because she had imagined being more of a recording artist, but her new outlook led her to an opportunity to audition for a production of the musical *Ain't Misbehavin'*. She got the job and was excited about being employed as a singer and getting to travel with the show. She also saw that this may very well be how her dream will come true. She is getting paid to use her gift, and succeeding at it could be her ticket to a recording contract as well. The quality of her life did not falter, even though she wasn't getting what she wanted right away. And that is what matters.

The higher the quality of your life remains as you move through the following steps, the easier your discovery and transition will be. Living your purpose and being *who* you want to be is your passport.

▶ Questions to Ponder

What would bring meaning to my life?

What does meaningful work mean to me?

What are the ways that people use me?

What is the theme to who I am, as seen through the eyes of others?

What is the essence of my dream?

In this chapter, what emerged as my purpose?

What can I do to turn up the volume on my purpose and start living it now?

What would the world be missing if I chose not to live from my purpose?

What kind of person would I like to be as I move forward in my life now?

What can I be doing now to start being who I want to be?

What have I learned about myself from this chapter?

Your Purpose Needs a Vehicle

*Nothing contributes so much to
tranquilizing the mind as a steady
purpose—a point on which the soul
may fix its intellectual eye.*
— MARY WOLLSTONECRAFT SHELLEY

It's time. We have done enough introspection, and now it is time
to start putting some form to all of your discoveries. We are now
holding some precious information that needs to be assimilated
and assigned to a new vehicle that can move you forward. Our
last step allowed us to find the essence of you, apart from the identity or packages you had attached yourself to. Previously, we dis-
sected thought patterns about what is really possible for you and
we drew out themes from your past that may inform your future.
In this chapter, we will determine new packages for your discoveries. In other words, what are all the possible ways you can move
forward in a new direction?

The biggest challenge this chapter will present to you is staying in *exploratory mode* and not letting logic or probability set in. It's not yet time for linear thinking. You are still exploring, although you are getting closer and closer to determining your direction and going for it. Suspending any judgment about the process and where it might lead you is necessary for success. You've been good about that so far, so just keep it up.

> ### Exercise: *Naming New "Packages"*

Take all the information you have gathered about yourself so far and study it by reading it over a few times. Based on your new insights about *who* you are, come up with a list of new *what*s. By that I mean make a list of all the possible packages (jobs, careers, roles) that your *who* could fit into. Allow your list to be as varied as possible. The only criterion is that the list include only things you would be attracted to doing. It's OK for now if they are far-fetched.

For example, if you discovered that your sense of purpose comes from being someone who can bring laughter to those that need it most, then your list of possible new packages could read like this:

Stand-up comedian

Public speaker

Medical professional

Current position as corporate manager

Advocate for the elderly

Kids' counselor

I worked with three wonderful people recently that all had the same through-line to the future they wanted to create. They all found a sense of purpose in making other people smile. Oddly, at that time none of them were in jobs that allowed them to do that. Jake, who we mentioned in Chapter One, was in media production. Jolie was a CFO of a small company and had just quit when she came to work with me. Nora was a longtime corporate executive who was trying to determine what her next move was for her career. When they had done as much of the process as you have now, they set out to make a list of professions that would allow them to make others smile. The following are their lists.

JAKE	JOLIE	NORA
Diplomat	Actor	Teacher
Lawyer	Adventure travel guide	Park ranger
Career/life coach	Animal trainer	Editor
Teacher	Antique dealer	Writer
Community relations director	Artist	Journalist
Personal trainer	Bridal store owner	Designer
Dietician	Clown	Store owner
Counselor/psychologist	Resort director	Gardener
Comedy writer	Counselor/therapist	Chef
Film producer	Decorator	Politician
Physical therapist	Beauty specialist	Historian
Hospital administrator	Florist	Librarian
Writer	Fund-raiser	Travel writer

JAKE	JOLIE	NORA
Lobbyist	Card/gift store owner	Banker
Politician	Wedding/party planner	Computer coach
Owner of a tutoring franchise	Park ranger	Animal trainer
Doctor	Massage therapist	
Entrepreneur in a helping field	Personal organizer	
FBI agent	Personal trainer	
Founder of charity	Writer	
	Travel agent	
	Ice-cream store owner	
	Golf coach	
	Teacher	

As you can see, the lists are varied. The options are many—almost too many. I will show you how to narrow the field shortly, but in the meantime, you might be curious to know what turned out to be the directions these three people chose.

Jake, after much consideration, felt that working with children, in a role where he could mentor them and help with their personal development, would be the right path for him. He knew it might take a while to make that change, but he felt he could stay in his current position knowing that he was headed to a brighter future. He began his transition by coaching his kid's T-ball team. It gave him tremendous satisfaction. His next step was to enroll in a training program to start shifting his skill set and experience to the new field he wanted to enter.

Jolie was headed toward working with a friend of hers in an event and wedding-planning business after also strongly considering becoming a personal organizer. She stopped herself short when she realized that these positions did not honor her financial skills and smarts. At the same time, she and her husband were beginning to look for a new place to live, and it suddenly hit her that the wheeling and dealing of real estate was right up her financial alley. She has since started to buy properties and fix them up for sale. She is making people smile by providing beautiful places to live!

Nora had a long list as well, but life showed her there was a new direction that did not come up on her list of packages. All the excavating we had done made a different kind of priority painfully clear. Nora had to settle some financial and emotional dealings with her immediate family before she could move her own life to a happier place. This new priority was really essential to moving her life forward. It would provide her with the financial and emotional freedom to really choose what she wanted for her life.

Nora came back to coaching a year later and picked up where we left off. The packages that were still relevant were those of travel writer and animal trainer. They still felt very far-fetched to her, considering her corporate background, but to get the ball rolling, she enrolled herself and her dog in an obedience-training course. As she pursued that, it occurred to her that she could combine travel writing and her love for her dog by specializing in locations that were pet-friendly. She began researching magazines for dog lovers to see if she could fill a gap by doing travel writing in that niche. It was an exciting idea that fit her so well that it begged to be explored. Nora envisioned it as a hobby at first, but was open to the possibility of what could happen along the way. This new idea fit her purpose of making others smile. All that mattered was that Nora's zest for life was coming back and there was something she could feel passionate about. Time will tell us the rest of the story.

Narrowing the Field

Now that you've let your imagination flow and have a list of possibilities, we are going to narrow the field. So far, it has been important to just let the ideas flow without editing or reality checks, to get the creative juices flowing. Now, we will begin to pepper in a little reality to see if you are really willing to reach for some of the things that sounded fun and interesting to you.

> **Exercise:** *Narrowing the Field*

Take your list of possible packages, and as you consider each one, ask yourself if it really interests you enough to keep it on the list. Do not use full-blown logic and get into the probability of doing these things just yet. Just a little dash of it will do. For example, Jolie had written down becoming a clown to make people smile. When she really tried to imagine herself doing that, clown school did not feel like a fit, so she eliminated it from her list.

Go down your list and eliminate the packages that you really don't see yourself committing to.

Let's say you are one of the people who is not using this process to discover your life's work or next career move, but rather are interested in moving your life forward based on some other criteria. For example, you might be considering moving to a new state or country or are looking for a new life partner or are considering what to do as you stare at your empty nest or are wondering whether the next step is starting a family or not. The same process applies. Instead of narrowing things down by profession, do so by situation.

The Research Project: Reality-Check Your Desires

Now the fun really begins, and it becomes critical that you created a structured schedule back in Chapter Two, because you will need to have time set aside on a daily basis to do this part of the process in order to move it along. It may very well need to continue into the subsequent weeks of the program. This part is called "The Research Project." I am going to put you on a research reconnaissance mission that will help with your process of elimination and help you determine which of your interests will truly become the future direction you will take.

The Research Project simply means that you will take the few final areas of interest that you have chosen and start researching them. Find people who are doing the same thing or have done the same thing in the past. Start putting on your investigator's hat and get down to separating reality from fantasy. Those who have gone before will shed light on your path and will help you sculpt and shape your direction. This is where a process of elimination and deductive reasoning become valuable tools for divining the future.

> ### Exercise: *The Research Project*

Take your list of possible directions and choose the first three you would like to start researching. Everyone you know is connected to plenty of other people, so keep asking around until you find people in the professions you are considering.

Speak to three people in each of these fields, and interview them about their experience and what it really takes to be in their place. Ask them how they got there, what it would take for you to break in (if it is a new field for you), what education or training you would need, and most important, what their day-to-day life is like doing what you are thinking of doing.

Eliminate possibilities from your list as it becomes clear that they are not "it," and replace them with new possibilities from your list until you have come up with one or two front-runners.

The research project can open unexpected doors and inspire creative new directions. Liz was a stay-at-home mom who I had worked with for a television segment. We only had eight weeks to work on her life together, instead of the twelve that you are getting, but we found "it" and put it into play as a reality. Liz wanted to figure out what she might do in a few years when she would be ready to get back into some kind of work. She wanted to use our time together to identify "it" and start retraining or preparing mentally to get back into the workforce.

Having previously worked her way up in an architecture firm, Liz felt she had been out of the job market a long time and needed to fully reinvent herself. She had no interest in going back to what she did before, but she really did not have any idea as to what to do next. The final few possibilities that came up on her list were: teacher of adults or high-school kids, nutritionist/dietitian, and owning her own business of some kind.

Liz got on the phone and started her research project. She spoke to teachers and got the scoop on what they face day in and day out. She learned about what kind of retraining she'd have to do to get her teaching certificate and what kind of hours she'd have to work to meet the criteria of the field. She decided teaching was not "it."

When she spoke to a few women business owners, she started to see how her nutritionist idea and owning her own business could be melded together. Liz's real motivation for writing down "nutritionist" was that she had an idea for working with families to get their kids to eat more healthy foods. She imagined being hired to consult with them, going to their homes and stripping their cabinets of the foods that kept their family on the "fat track." She would then help them create a weekly grocery list that brought healthier meals and snacks into their home. Liz felt strongly that most parents needed to be better educated about nutrition, but she feared she did not have the credentials to do this. She thought she would need to train as a nutritionist or dietitian. One of her business-owner contacts, however, showed her how she could begin right away.

Liz brainstormed with her new friend and came up with something she wanted to do right away that did not require a license, a degree, or a self-imposed wait of a few years until her children were in school. "The Lunch Bunch," as it was called, was an activity that moms could participate in with their kids; they would do fun projects with healthy foods and then eat them for lunch. Each mom would pay a reasonable fee for the class and lunch, and would get a fun activity to do with her kids that resulted in healthy eating. Liz would get to start a business in her home that included her children and use it as a start to the nutrition consulting she'd like to do.

I attended the first Lunch Bunch, where Liz guided the children in making clown faces out of soft flour wraps, rice, and freshly cut, lightly steamed vegetables. The mothers chuckled, thinking that their kids would never eat the healthy stuff, and then stood in amazement as the kids ate their clowns, veggies and all.

Liz was amazed at how fast she went from having no idea how she would reenter the working world to actually being in business in eight weeks' time. She worked on a great logo for her business and saw how she could fit in time to retrain as a nutritionist.

Like Liz's story and several others you'll read, the research project will lead you to unexpected opportunities and insights. For some of you, the momentum will accelerate, and "it" will become evident by the doors that open to you. For others, it may not move as fast, but you will move forward. It's like working at a potter's wheel. The clay slowly takes on a shape that becomes more and more defined as the artist works. You are the artist, and you are shaping the form that your life will take with each new discovery. All it takes is patience and a balance of precision and experimentation.

Six Degrees of Separation

Everyone you want to meet is supposed to be no more than six people away from you, right? In doing your research project, you'll probably find that they are closer than you think. If you don't know someone firsthand who does what you are looking to investigate, then someone you know can probably lead you to someone who does. The magic is in the asking. And the key to successful asking is being specific. For example:

Who do you know who works in _____?

Who can you connect me to who may be able to shed some light on becoming a _____?

Can you help me find someone who could share their expertise in _____?

Do you know anyone who has _____?

I know you are smart enough to figure this out yourself, but I also know how paralyzing it can be to seriously consider your options at this point. Sometimes it feels like there are so many options that it is overwhelming. Other times, the reality that you are too far into making a change to *not* make one can be daunting, too. There is also the possibility that you have yet to connect passionately to something and feel as though you are passively doing what I ask. That is uncomfortable, too. Whether your mood reflects any of these situations or you are totally psyched to do your research, just get on with it. The process of elimination and the discoveries you'll make through your research might surprise you.

> **The Reality-Check Conversation**

Here's a reality-check conversation checklist. Whether by appointment, phone, fax, or e-mail, ask your interviewee the inside scoop on what they do for a living.

Field/Situation I am researching: _____

Who is my contact: _____ Phone Number: _____

E-mail: _____

(Continued)

Exercise *(Continued)*

How did you get where you are today? _____

_____

What training would I need before considering getting into this field?

_____

What could I expect as a beginning point in this arena? _____

What is the best part of what you do? _____

_____

What are the headaches of what you do? _____

_____

What are your complaints?_____

_____

What is the inside reality of your situation vs. the way people perceive
it from the outside? _____

_____

What are the pitfalls of what you do? _____

_____

What kind of income could I expect early on? _____

What is meaningful for you about what you do/about your situation?

_____

If you had it to do all over again, what would you do differently?

_____

What advice do you have for someone like me? _____

_____

While you focus on the three situations at a time, and as you complete each reality-check conversation, take a moment to imagine yourself in that profession or life situation based on the information you have gathered. Ask yourself how it feels. If it's exciting and scary, it stays on the list. If the reality negates your fantasy, and it no longer has any emotional appeal, you have your answer.

It doesn't matter at this point if you cannot imagine how you would make a transition to this new profession or life situation. That should not enter into your decision about what stays on your list. You will soon read stories of amazing ways that people crossed over to new situations. At the time, they, too, could not see how they would get from one thing to another. Right now, that is not your concern. Stick with your research project. Just one step at a time, please.

Not knowing how to get into a new field can be nerve-wracking, but it also creates room for pleasant surprises. Jean was a client who got very anxious upon discovering that she had a strong desire to work within the adoption field. She and her husband had adopted a child a few years before, and as we explored the packages she might pursue, her interest in adoption burned brighter. She wasn't sure if she would want to be a family advocate, run an adoption agency, or run a not-for-profit organization. She was simultaneously wondering how she would move from a 25-year career in wholesale high-fashion footwear to one of these jobs, and she almost imploded trying to make sense of it all. I warned her, as I just warned you, that all she needed to do was work on her research project and have the reality-check conversations. She did not have to know if this was "it" or figure out how she might make the switch.

"We know we are headed east," I said. "We just don't know which city we are going to and what time we will arrive."

Wouldn't you know that as Jean innocently talked to people about what it would mean to work in the adoption world, she found out about two organizations that worked to provide orphans and their caretakers around the world with shoes! *Ta-da!* A connection between adoption and shoes! Jean saw these organizations as instant opportunities to contribute. She had so many contacts in her industry that she knew it could make a difference for these agencies. She saw an opening that she knew she needed to enter. She had a hunch that the adoption world was "it," and she saw the shoe project as a great way to get started.

Jean was able to calm down and see that not every step needed to be certain and planned, and that she could stay at her current job while she continued to explore her new area of interest.

But I'm Not Qualified

Different fears crop up at different times during this process, but one that might appear now is the "but I'm not qualified to do that" fear. When people start seeing possible new directions and gather the information about entering new fields, it is inevitable that they'll wonder what gives them the gall to even consider these new options. You're normal, OK? However, you are mistaken if you are going to let it stop you. When you enter the space where the answers start coming in as to what is next in your life, you have begun to operate on a level that is beyond the rules of normal accomplishment. We are accessing the realm of *who* you are, not *what* you are, and that means you are qualified for much more than the world around you may recognize.

I know I enter fragile territory when I say that book knowledge and educational degrees are not the only proof that someone knows what they are doing. Natural talent and knowledge that you cannot trace to specific training count for something, and sheer passion and excitement cannot be undervalued. Granted, I would not want the pilot of a plane I'm in, or a surgeon who is about to cut me open, to be operating on sheer passion alone, but in this stage of discovery, qualifications cannot be a reason to stop. The true obstacles will become clear. You do not have to create obstacles that say you can't before you even try.

What is necessary is to develop the skills you will need to go into something else—but not necessarily the title or degree. Where to attain those skills will vary from formal training to apprenticeship to volunteering to reading up and self-study. If retraining does become something you have to do, you will find a way to fit it into your life. Keep your options open through the research project, and let each reality-check conversation become a piece of the puzzle. Some pieces will fit as the picture of your direction comes into focus, and some pieces will not fit at all. Your research will make it clear.

> ### ▶ Questions to Ponder

What did I learn about myself from this chapter?

What are the most likely packages for my purpose?

What are some early outcomes of my research project?

What scares me most about my discoveries?

What am I excited about?

What kind of retraining might I need to consider?

What's possible now?

Your Criteria for Happiness: Is This Really "It"?

Happiness is the state of consciousness which proceeds from the achievement of one's values.

—AYN RAND

What have you got? Just as each Halloween I sit with anticipation, waiting to see which of my favorite candies my kids will bring home from trick-or-treating, I now sit wondering what your research project yielded for you. What came to the top of the barrel? What are the directions you are excited about and starting to lose sleep over? I hope clarity is becoming yours.

Assuming that your research project allowed you to narrow down the possible directions for your life, you are now entering a point where you can check what you found against the criteria you started to develop earlier in the process. This will help you align what interests you with your Life Blueprint. Chances are they are perfectly aligned, but in case you have any concern about whether you are on the right track, this chapter should make it undeniably clear.

Name "It"

What is "it"? What has become the undeniable truth? What do you now know you have to do or include in your life? Some of you will see a clear-cut career choice or life direction. For others, it will be a strong theme or personal quality that needs to become the obvious focus of your life. Either one qualifies as a direction. If it begs for attention, you know deep down you must integrate it and honor the truth you have excavated, and, for the most part, you are ready to do "it."

Don't let "how" questions get in your way. It's OK if it's not clear how you would do something, or how you would get from one thing to another or explain it to your spouse or your neighbors or bosses. That is not the priority at the moment. What is the priority is giving "it" a name. What's next for you?

For some of you, this will be easy. For others, it may strike panic in your heart, especially if your research project did not yield anything indicative of a clear direction. If that is the case for you, or if you are still feeling stuck, this would be a good time to take a break from this process. Go back to the earlier chapters and see what you might have overlooked. If you find that more frustrating than helpful, take a break altogether. Focus on improving and upgrading your day-to-day life. Take care of any glaring outstanding personal issues that need attention and that you may have been trying to override by doing this work. I warned that this could be the case earlier in the book. If you thought it did not apply to you and now you find yourself stuck, you have to ask yourself the hard questions about what is not working in your life and go back and work on those questions. Clarity will come when some of those issues are resolved. There is a natural order to life, and when we don't heed it, it can cause pain. Take care of yourself and your immediate life first. Then focus on dreams, goals, and creating a fabulous future.

Most of you are moving on with me here. Don't be surprised if you are feeling somewhat mellow at this point. You've learned a lot about yourself, and that can be exhausting. Also, the sexiness of early discoveries may have matured into a sobering reality, and that is fine. Even if you are moving forward but are not really sure about an "it" or feel that you are still dancing with a couple of "it"s, continue on. In case you have any doubts, the following stories should help you see the level of clarity needed to move on. It doesn't need to be perfect and include a plan. It just needs to be an undeniable truth that you can bathe in possibility and feel excited about making a reality.

Clarity came for Feroza, the woman you read about in Chapter Three who had become a lawyer to gain independence from her family situation. She came out of her search knowing that moving her part-time art studies to full-time was what was next for her. We had brainstormed many ideas of how she could get financial support to do that, and although she did not leave the 90 days established in her studies with full sponsorship, she knew this was her direction nonetheless. She knew she would find a way.

Another example of how far along you might be is Karen, from Chapter One, who really wanted her own business but felt a VP position was a prerequisite. She got to this point and admitted that having her own business had become the undeniable next step. In fact, knowing this caused her some dismay because she now knew she had to act on it. This was what was next, and not the VP position. Again, she wasn't sure how or what or when, but her direction was set.

Jake knew it was working with kids. Jean knew it had something to do with adoption. Lucy, who you'll hear about shortly, knew it was the freedom to enjoy and pursue photography, even if she kept her large PR firm. (She entered the process wondering if she could really do both.)

I hope you can see that the expectation at this point is not that you have a vision for the rest of your life or how you will get to the other side of your new dream. I would like to know that you can name it and claim it as the truth for yourself. Many people report feeling relieved at this stage. At least you know what "it" is. A lot of folks find a renewed zest for their life, even though nothing much has changed yet. If they have to stay in their current position or situation longer, they are still at ease because they have a new horizon to focus on.

Where Should the Passion Lie? A Hobby or Your Life's Work?

To defuse another possible trigger to letting your rational mind lead you off track from your blueprint, I'd like to address an issue that could come up now. Many a client and workshop participant has asked me, "How do you know that the thing that comes up as 'it' is supposed to become your work or if it's just meant to be a hobby you are passionate about?" Good question. But it's usually my job to ask the questions, so here it goes. Are you willing to make the sacrifices it would take to do that thing as your livelihood (or main focus)?

Some of you will answer with a resounding yes, others a clear no, and still others won't be so sure. Money and lifestyle will have a lot to do with your decision. The entire next chapter will be on money and helping you gain clarity about your financial situation. For now, let us focus on the generalities of adopting your passion as your life's work.

In Chapter Two, we took stock of what you had to mourn and let go of in order to move forward. We are much further along here, and if you are up against a difficult choice as to whether or not to make the change that has moved to the forefront, it's time to measure potential loss again. It will help you determine how far you are willing to go to integrate your new direction. Taking a look at what you may have to give up is also helpful if you have ever started comparing yourself to other people. (Who hasn't?) It will shift your perception to realize that it's not about asking yourself why you don't have what they have, but rather considering what you would have to give up to get where they are and if you are truly willing to do that.

If you are indeed wondering whether you are looking at a hobby or a clear life direction, the next exercise will help. Remember, this exercise will fit other situations as well. To go back to school or not, to marry a sweetheart or not, to extricate yourself from a relationship or not, and many others can be measured here, too.

▶ **Exercise:** *What Are You Giving Up?*

What do you have to give up? Take pen to paper and write down what you would have to give up, stop doing, and have

(Continued)

Exercise *(Continued)*

less of (or more of) in order to bring this new possible direction into reality. Then write down what you would gain to go in that direction. Take some time to imagine what life would be like if it were reoriented with your interest as its main focus.

When you are done, ask yourself if you still want it at the forefront of your life. Fear would be normal and appropriate here, but that's not a reason to stop yourself from moving forward. More concrete logistics and life changes would qualify as reasons to reconsider.

For example: Chris, a Frisbee champion in his spare time, considered getting further sponsorship to go full-time but recognized that the travel and time commitment would make him a long-distance father, something he could not live with.

On the other hand, Janine was so passionate about fitness that she felt she could live with the loss of her dependable job and paycheck in order to be involved in her passion full-time. She eventually made her living in the fitness world.

Not everyone is cut out for dramatic change, so volunteering, experimenting, or hobbying all become viable options. If your research project only touched the surface, enough to make this choice come to the forefront but not enough to propel you into pursuing it, you may need to do an expanded version of your research project and actually get involved in your choice for a while. Having an experience in a limited time frame that allows you to experiment with what it would mean to move your life in that direction might be helpful. It might propel you to make the change, or to simply recognize that you don't need to do this thing full-time and that it was never meant to be more than a hobby.

Lucy, who I mentioned briefly earlier, owns a very successful public relations firm and is a high-profile businesswoman in her community. She felt very tethered to her business, and, being a single mom, felt there was really no way to entertain any other options of full-time passion and focus. For years, Lucy complained that if she really had her way, she would do something with photography. Upon entering the 90-day process, she suddenly determined that she was sick of hearing herself complain. She arranged her life to have one day off a week from the office, went to the local newspaper, and told them she would volunteer once a week to be on call to them for photo journalism. They agreed, and she launched her experiment to find out if the angst of not doing her photography was a calling to a new life direction or just a creative outlet that she needed to give credence to.

Lucy could finally stop beating herself up for not trying photography. Just a few weeks into her experiment, she was clear that her craft was only to be a hobby. She did not feel any pull to do more with it, but she had answered a perennial question at last. She started adding more time in her schedule to take pictures, and she is working on a couple of photo essays for her own enjoyment.

Lisa, on the other hand, was one of the people who experimented her way right into a new career. For years, she had worked as a professional makeup artist for commercials and movies. Her work required short stints away from home and her children, which was fine while her husband was around. Finding herself suddenly separated and going through a divorce, she was at a loss as to what to do to make a living in a way that did not require travel. She was just not willing to leave her children anymore.

Having always been very creative when it came to decorating and making decorative items for her home, Lisa looked at who she wanted to be in her life (supportive of others, turning people on to beauty) and the things that people reflected about her (that she was creative and had great taste), she recognized that doing interior design was a package that matched her blueprint. Worried that she had no credentials and wasn't trained, she blocked herself from moving forward for a while, until she realized she had nothing to lose by just trying.

Lisa started by helping some friends redo rooms in their homes at no charge. They were so pleased that she became more serious about making money at her new career choice. She researched suppliers and got her resources together. She set up an official business and got her paperwork in order. She named it Metamorphosis. She designed a list of services—everything from rearranging and redesigning rooms in people's homes using their existing belongings to full-design services including designing, shopping, and executing the concepts for people's homes.

In hardly any time at all, Lisa was up and running, and earning what she needed to support herself and her family. She was used to working freelance, as she had as a makeup artist, so the risk came in making a name for herself in something she feared she was inexperienced with. Her courage paid off.

Path vs. Analogy

Is it a path to follow or is it an analogy? In further considering if something is supposed to be a hobby or a full-time pursuit, a question has been helpful to my clients: Is the something that occurs to you (or that your intuition has brought to your awareness) a path you are meant to follow, or an analogy for something you are meant to include or transform in some way? If there is no clear answer to that question, the only way to find out is to try it.

If what you sense as a direction is an analogy for something, you could try to transform your current situation in some way to reflect what you know. For example, Max was a very successful executive who had a nagging desire to start his own business. The reality of that pursuit was daunting to him. He made a great income and had so much he liked about his life that the thought of starting from scratch was almost intolerable. He was truly conflicted because the desire just would not dissipate. Was this desire really supposed to be his next step, a path to follow, or was it an analogy for something else?

In considering what this direction might mean as an analogy, Max had an aha. His round face became animated and childlike as he saw that he needed to treat his current position more like it was his own business. He needed to ask for more autonomy, take more risks, and let some of his more innovative ideas be known. He recognized that he had been keeping his ideas to himself and becoming disgruntled because of them. He realized that if he rewrote his job description, asking for more responsibility, and became more vocal in meetings with his bosses, he could start to shift some of his boredom and ennui. He saw where he needed to "own" the business he was already doing by investing in it emotionally with all that he had.

Max felt such a relief to see that he did not have to jump ship from his job right away. He was ready to enthusiastically return to his current position. He understood that he would take this approach, and that it may be exactly the experience he needs to start a business someday. He also saw that if he is indeed meant to have his own business, it would become painfully obvious as he went on.

Your Criteria for Happiness

Have you thought about your criteria for happiness? "Criteria? For happiness?" you might ask. It sounds strange, but it is those who know what makes them happy who know how to be happy. You might assume that the opposite is true. You might assume that if you feel happy, you're happy, period, and the circumstances don't matter. When you have criteria for happiness, usually collected through experience, you can multiply your chances for happiness by making sure you honor the criteria through the choices that life presents you with. Your criteria for happiness give you higher odds for finding the peace of being who you really are. As Johnny Carson, longtime TV host of *The Tonight Show*, once said: "If you're happy in what you are doing, you'll like yourself, you'll have inner peace. And if you have that, along with physical health, you will have had more success than you could possibly have imagined."

You chose the professions and situations for your research project based on your list of who you wanted to be as you move forward and build that on the discovery of your sense of purpose or recognizing your natural abilities. That is a huge part of being aligned with your Life Blueprint. Before committing to taking action or accepting an opportunity that comes up, it will be helpful to have your criteria handy as a checklist to measure your decisions against. You already have your list of who you want to be as you move forward. Any move you make needs to reflect your list or you will quickly tire or outgrow the new situation. It is also easy to be seduced by something that looks like an opportunity in the conventional "get ahead" sense but, on closer look, is out of line with your blueprint. The next two inquiries will help you make wise decisions.

Needs and Values

At opposite ends of the spectrum from each other are your needs and your values. Your needs are those things that are not optional and that are highly critical to you feeling at ease in your world. A need for honesty, recognition, or productivity, for example, is something that needs to be present for you to feel OK. Wired in you, thanks to your early life experiences, your needs are those things that drive you nuts if they are not present in your life.

Your values, on the other hand, are the pot of gold at the end of the rainbow. They are the things that would make your life idyllic, the things most people think they will have to wait until they retire or get their kids out of the house or be older or wiser to enjoy—for example, finding that it is important for you to include spirituality, teaching, influence, or luxury, which become the infusion of heaven that you've been longing to include in your life. Needs and values therefore become two more lenses to see your life's decisions through. I've outlined the different characteristics of both to better make the distinction for you.

Needs	Values
Negatively charged until met	Positively charged
Drive you/push you	Naturally drawn to them
Can bring out the sides of you that you don't like	Feel like home; bring out your best

NEEDS	VALUES
Happiness depends on them	Happiness enhanced by them
Need to have them	Like to have them

> ### Exercise: *"Need" and "Values"*

Ask yourself what brings you satisfaction but needs to be refueled by certain actions or situations. Those would be needs for you. Write down three needs that fit the preceding criteria that you know are not optional to you feeling that things are right with your world. *Examples:* to be heard, included, recognized, accomplished, or the best, or to have control, stability, certainty, autonomy, luxury, perfection, or results.

Then ask yourself what gives you a sustainable, healthy, peaceful feeling and is not that dependent on day-to-day circumstances. These are your values—not your moral and ethical values as much as your internal triggers for feeling well and right. *Examples:* adventure, grace, beauty, excellence, leading, inspiring, creating, designing, performing, spirituality, teaching, service, advocacy, style, and discovery.

Notice the duality working within you. When you can create a balance between the two, you will experience satisfaction in your life.

These distinctions were very important to me back when I was suffering about what else I might do with my life. Once I saw that a life in the theatre was not the life I thought it would be, I had no criteria for deciphering what might be next. It was so confusing at the time, because I had no idea that my needs were driving me.

I had a high need for recognition, which is probably what drove me to pursue theatre and acting in the first place. Besides being good at it, it fed a hungry, needy place inside me. The problem was that I was too dependent on getting hired and being given an opportunity to perform to have that need met. It was going to be fed only by circumstances that often stood too far out of my control. When I realized that the need for recognition drove many of my actions, I was able to make more conscious choices about how I could meet that need. Instead of it driving me, I began to make choices about it.

I learned that I needed to recognize myself and acknowledge more of my own day-to-day accomplishments instead of always waiting for some form of recognition from the outside. When I did, the need calmed down. I still lead a life where there is plenty of recognition from the outside world, but I have changed the balance of power. I can live without it. Before, I couldn't.

When you analyze your needs, recognize that they don't have to run your life. You can make wiser decisions about how those needs get met once you recognize that they are there. You may still choose to have them met by your work or relationships, but you can do more to meet them yourself once you know their names. As a basic rule, every time there is an upset in your life, ask yourself which need is not being met. If you can answer that question, you'll have access to a quicker, longer-lasting solution.

Michael had a critical need to be included. At his job, he seemed to be at the fringe of the crowd that seemed to be in the know about the internal workings at the company. He assumed he was not included for some specific reason, and the longer he was excluded from lunches, after-work drinks, or hallway conversations, the more aggravated he became. When he could name the need—being included—he saw that he did not have to wait to be invited into this group to meet his need, and that he did not have to behave like an outsider, either. The next time he saw these people in the hallway, he joined them. Despite months of feeling left out and somehow colluded against, he found that no one seemed to mind that he included himself in the group. People easily welcomed him and even started to ask him to join in their impromptu lunch outings. He met the need by taking action himself and not waiting for someone to meet it for him. But first he needed to name it.

Matthew was a client whose situation will give you a glimpse of how to recognize your values. Matthew came to realize why he was always volunteering to lead projects and programs in his community when he named "inspiring" as one of his values. He just loved volunteering, and was lit up by it and almost could not help himself from raising his hand every time a committee needed someone to drive an effort. The rough part, however, was that Matthew wondered why he did not feel the same way at work. He had a very technical job where he tended to work alone. It wasn't until we named "inspiring" as a value that he realized he had to include it more in his life. His job wasn't really designed for him to have a chance to lead, but he did participate in a volunteer task force on his job that put him in front of the right people, and eventually he was recognized as someone who could inspire others. Over the course of a year, he was able to keep his eye on internal job postings, and he kept educating his superiors on what kinds of things he'd like to be doing. He was able to transfer to a different department, still using his technical abilities, but also putting him in touch with more people so he could lead and inspire. He was so much happier at work, and as you can imagine, it touched all parts of his life.

Values light you up. They are also hardwired in you like your needs are, but needs will tend to be louder and hungrier, and will block your way to living from your values. Once your needs are taken care of, your values will become clearer and more attainable. They will also evolve to feel like they are not optional. When you hear people say that they can no longer work at a certain place because it does not match their values, you are hearing people who have excavated their way to the truth about themselves that they can no longer deny. Their values become their principles to live by, and they don't feel quite right if they ignore them.

To review, you have criteria now for which possible directions will make you happy. Do they allow you to be all of who you are? Do they allow you to be *who* you want to be and *who* you want to become? Can you tap a sense of purpose through them? Can you get your needs met and honor your values? If you can answer these questions affirmatively, you've crossed over to the other side. You've gone from lost to found, or from out of focus to focused.

Congratulations are in order. You have completed the first half of this program. You have an "it." "It" may be a clear-cut direction, career choice, or life decision. "It" may also be an inspiring discovery that still needs to take form. "It" may be an aha for you, or you've might of known all along, but I have no doubt that you have more clarity than you did when you began this process. Now it is time to turn that clarity into action and an outcome. Hold on to your hat. Here we go.

▶ Questions to Ponder

What's next?

What's my "it"?

Is my "it" a path or an analogy?

What are my critical needs?

What are my values?

What are my criteria for happiness?

What is concerning me about moving forward?

What have I learned about myself from this chapter?

Part II

Getting There
(Weeks 8–12)

Chapter Eight

The Bottom Line Is the Bottom Line

*The real measure of your wealth is how
much you'd be worth if you lost all
your money.*

—ANONYMOUS

Money. It is such a loaded topic for so many people. In essence,
the bottom line *is* the bottom line when it comes to being willing
to make a change. Fear, doubts, and lack of training are molehills
compared to the stopping power of the mountain we call money.
Hey, if you have any doubts about moving forward with your life,
you can always blame your inertia on money. Oddly enough, it
isn't always a lack of money that stops us. Often, it is the abundance of it. "If I make a change, can I make the same money?"
Most of us are just not willing to alter our external lifestyle to
enhance our inner life with satisfaction and fulfillment. Are we
really ready to make happiness the bottom line?

Many in our culture have come to define having less or downsizing our lifestyle as failure. Yet we often congratulate those that
have the courage to do it, because we don't. The question then

becomes: What exactly would we be failing at? I guess we would be failing at remaining competitive, and we'd be failing at sustaining appearances. Some could say they are failing to fulfill the obligation established by the precedent they have set as an earner of a certain caliber. We often become afraid of letting down family and friends who rely on our status or income for certain comforts in their lives. This applies to career changes as well as changes in marital status. So many people stay together to keep a lifestyle. Whether one partner is afraid that they can't make it on their own or, on the other hand, afraid of the financial ramifications of a split. Do any of these define you?

Besides the external obstacles that cause us shame or fear, there is a much more significant obstacle that keeps us stuck. That is the fear many of us have of actually taking responsibility for our finances and really looking at what we have or don't have. In this chapter, I'm going to help you look at and take charge of your finances. Half of it may feel like torture but, as your mother might have said, "It's good for you!" The other half will be a new twist you may have never thought of before.

So many clients of mine have put me in the position of figuratively holding a gun to their heads to get them to sit down and assess their financial situations. It's so much easier not to know. People are afraid that they'll find things are worse than they thought. Many, in the end, are surprised to find it's not as bad as they'd assumed. But knowing your situation is crucial to making your next step a reality.

Katie was one of those people who would have preferred not to look at her money for as long as she could. She was a stylist for catalog shoots and commercials who had a passion for art and dreamed of being a curator of an art museum or gallery someday. She took frequent trips to other countries to meet artists and bring home their work. She often sold several of the pieces, but kept her interest as a hobby only. She felt she just did not have the money to pursue things further, but she did come to me to design a plan to cross over to her new desired career in the course of the next four years.

If money was Katie's obstacle, then she needed to know her opponent and face it square-on. After much cajoling, she finally sat down and looked at her money situation. For her, it was a little worse than she thought, but she found that *knowing* was more of a relief than not knowing. She had allowed herself to not know for too long.

Katie tracked her expenses so she could know what she was spending. She saw that putting her business and home expenses on the same credit card was a mistake, so she took steps to separate them. She also got a separate account for her art business. She organized her paperwork accordingly and started using a computer program to keep better track of it all. By knowing what she had, she was able to cut back on some expenses (like eating out every day) and was able to stockpile some savings to use on her next trip to buy art. Also, for the first time, Katie put numbers to what she wanted her monthly income to be and started to pursue work more proactively instead of waiting for the phone to ring.

When my work with Katie was done, she was well on her way to making art her full-time passion and livelihood. She came to me in the hopes of creating a four-year plan, but in the end it turned out to be a three-month plan. By the time we wrapped up, she had found a new place to live within her means that had space for an art gallery right in her home. She gave up the notion of being a curator someday, and instead started to show her collections to interior designers and individuals who bought art on the spot. She started delegating more of her stylist work to assistants, and made the mental shift that she was an art dealer who did styling as a supplement instead of being a stylist who sometimes sold art. It may still take her a few years to build her reputation and business to a point of being self-sustaining, but she was already glowing with the satisfaction of making her vision a reality. Being on such a solid track changed her whole outlook, which only improved her business in tangible ways.

Knowing Is Better Than Not Knowing

You've got to know, so there is no better time than now to take a look at your money. Dig out those files, receipts, and statements, and get to work! Figure out what you have and what you owe. Get an accurate picture of your financial whereabouts. As painful as it is for many investors in times of global economic softness, you have to get a vivid picture of what is corralled in your name so you can make a more educated plan for what's next. It's hard to make things better if you don't have an accurate picture of what you are up against.

> ### Exercise: *It's Time to Know*

Did you think I was kidding? Here is your chance to assess your financial situation as an assignment.

Dig out all your financial statements and reconcile your checking account, savings account, life insurance, stocks, mutual funds, bonds, annuities, loans, mortgages, lines of credit, credit cards, tax bills, and any other income-producing or -reducing activities.

Make an assessment of how much money you have and

how much you owe. Take a good, honest look at your money. The following checklist will help.

ASSETS

Cash on hand: _____

Checking account balances: _____

Savings account balances: _____

Credit union balance: _____

IRA, SEP, pension plans: _____

Stock portfolio (current market value): _____

Bonds: _____

Life insurance (cash value): _____

House/apartment: _____

Auto/motorcycle/boat (cash value): _____

Collections and collectibles: _____

Art: _____

Furnishings (cash value): _____

Clothing (cash value): _____

Equipment: _____

Accounts receivable (money owed to you): _____

Tax refunds due: _____

Other: _____

Total assets: _____

(Continued)

Exercise *(Continued)*

LIABILITIES

Current bills: _____

Bills in arrears: _____

Mortgage or rent payments: _____

Credit card balances: _____

Credit line balances: _____

Installment loan balances: _____

Personal debts: _____

Child support/alimony: _____

Student loans: _____

Taxes owed: _____

Other liabilities: _____

_____

Total liabilities: _____

Total assets: _____

Total liabilities: − _____

                                                  _____

Net worth: _____

Where Does It Go?

Now that you've accounted for what you have, let's account for where it goes. It is so easy to spend and not really know where all your money goes. So many of our purchases are intangible—eating out, coffee on the run, kids' activities, services like dry cleaning and housekeepers and other things we enjoy. However, these are not objects we hold, feel, touch, and use for a long period of time, and they can be easy to forget about keeping track of. It is these miscellaneous items that keep us guessing where our money goes.

> ▶ **Exercise:** *Keeping Track*
>
> Buy a small pocket notebook and carry it out around with you this week to record every cent you spend. Car fare, the morning paper, gas, lunch, a keep-the-kids-quiet-so-you-can-shop purchase, and all the things you probably don't think twice about.
>
> After the week is over, add up everything by categories and try to estimate what the cost of those things would add up to per month. It's ideal to do this for a month while you are working on the other chapters, to give the most accurate count. The predictions based on one week will help us take a first stab at your budget.

Over the years, many clients and workshop participants have scoffed at keeping track of what they spend and creating a budget. Most of the time, the source of their complaints is that doing so makes them feel constrained. I retort by saying that knowing what you spend, and what you need to spend to live the way you want to, is less of a restraint and more of a device for freedom. A budget is a structure to create *from*. It gives you scope and boundaries, and it gives you the freedom to choose. It allows you to decide to spend or not to spend, and decide how you want to live instead of just reacting as life demands. It measures your values and what is important to you, and lets you see how money can help you achieve your goals. Staying in the dark about your money is what is constraining. You don't know what you don't know, and there is little room to imagine your financial situation becoming any different. *Knowing* makes the case for change. Awareness is the first step.

The Budget

Simply put, the budget is your measuring system. It helps you measure how much of the pie has to go to each item that makes up the life you lead. If you measure it correctly, you will have enough for the whole pie. If you overmeasure and put too much in some areas and not enough in others, you will mix the crust with the filling, and you'll start to have a mess on your hands.

What do you need to live the life you live? That's the first question. Then we will concern ourselves with what you need for the new direction you are toying with. It may mean cutting back, or it may mean living on savings for a while. But first things first. Let's measure where it all goes.

> ### ▶ Exercise: *Budgeting*
>
> Start with your fixed monthly expenses—those things you can rely on getting a regular bill for. The rent or mortgage,

car payment, utility bills, day-care costs, groceries—you know the drill. Take out your checkbook and look at what you regularly write checks for. Record those categories as your fixed monthly expenses. (Check your bank statement for ATM or debit withdrawals that come up monthly, too.)

Next, you'll need to track your less-regular expenses like insurance, taxes, clothes, cleaning bills, quarterly maintenance fees, or unexpected repairs to your home or cars. Try to look at the last year to estimate roughly what those less-regular expenses are on average.

Look at all your categories and add up the numbers. You are looking at the nut.

I know that budgeting is basic stuff, but it never hurts to check in. You are going to need the whole picture to begin the creative process of financing the change you have in mind. With this information, we will determine later in this chapter if you are going to need to reduce your expenses or make some other arrangements. For now, we'll take some time off from the drill to peel back the layers of the onion with respect to money and your Life Blueprint.

The "Who" of Money

Money is such a powerful tool in our lives. Not only can it alter our creature comforts and access to services and things that we want, but it also can alter us emotionally, mentally, and spiritually. Money can transform you as a person. It would be easier if that were not the case and if we could remain composed regardless of the lack or abundance of money in our life. But the truth is, much of us have "stuff" around money: behaviors, fears, hang-ups, very rigid opinions, or a set of values. What I really want to know, however, is how money affects you. Does it allow you to be who you want to be, or does it cause you to become someone you'd rather not be? Remember our exercise about who you want to be as you move forward from your discovery of your sense of purpose? How does money help you or hinder you from that list of qualities?

> **Exercise:** *The "Who"*

Take pen to paper and write about *who* money allows you to be in your life. Who does it allow you to be with other people, who does it allow you to be in your world? Write about the positive aspects of your life and personality that exists thanks to money. Second, write about who money causes you to be that you do not like. Third, explore and write about who you'd like to be as you move forward with your attitude about money.

For example, money may allow you to feel powerful and free. It may also cause you to feel anxious and lonely if you are someone who avoids being with friends because you are afraid of not being able to keep up with them finan-cially. Moving forward, you may like to be someone who uses money as a tool and who is free from the fears it makes you operate from.

Look at your answers to see how healthy or unhealthy your relationship is to money. We will use this information to move you forward very shortly.

If you feel you have a healthy relationship to money, then you will probably be more flexible when it comes to making a change in your life. If your *who* is adversely affected by money, you may have a tougher time.

When you don't let money define you, it's likely that you'll get through financial crisis with more ease. Doug was someone who has been able to do very well financially at times in his life, and at other times, he has had more modest and sometimes scarce years. Of course, he enjoys the good times, but he seems reasonably un-affected emotionally when the low times come around. He re-mains steady and focused, and does not lose or gain self-esteem as his bank account fluctuates. He always remains confident that the good times will come back, and he takes action to guarantee it. He by no means goes into denial or passiveness to deal with his money problems. He does what he needs to do to turn it around, and since he saves money when he is doing well, he has a cush-ion to get through the rockier times.

Al, on the other hand, is someone who will keep his lifestyle high and, by appearances, glamorous, even if things are not going well. Appearances are everything to him, so he will go into debt and become more and more agitated as money fluctuates in his life. He is never willing to give anything up when he faces tough times, and over the years, his health has started to show stress-related wear and tear.

It's not about having or not having as much as it is about how money or the lack of makes you feel. Two women, Colleen and Andrea, are people in my life who I observe quietly when it comes to their attitudes about money. One makes a little more than the other. Both have families and live in suburban areas. Colleen, who makes a little more, always has something new to wear or to show off in her home, but she always talks about how tight money is for her, and she can't even consider making charitable contributions. Andrea makes a bit less, and has paid less attention to her home and her wardrobe, but considers herself so lucky that she donates her money often to spread her feelings of good fortune. Putting aside any judgment or assessment about how they live, I would like to point out their different relationships to money. Colleen seems to use fear as a motivator to keep making more. The more insecure she feels, the better, because she pushes herself to make more. Andrea has her moments of fear that she won't have things that she wants, or that she may suffer a difficult time, but she usually feels very good about herself, her life, and her money. Which would you rather embody?

You may not be at such extremes as Doug and Al, or Colleen and Andrea, but now would be a good time to make some conscious choices about how you would like to behave when it comes to money. Fear can be a great motivator, but life would be easier if you could find a different source of inspiration. To let your Life Blueprint carry you to a place that will make you happy and satisfied, you have to bring money into perspective. It has to become a tool and not a means to an end. It must be transformed for you into something you are in partnership with instead of something that you are trying to conquer or that you have been afraid of. It is part of the journey, but not the destination. This may require concrete changes to your lifestyle, but primarily it requires an internal shift—one that can manifest when you discover the place where you got out of sync with money and then guide your relationship with money to how you would like it to be.

Facing Your Past Mistakes, Financing Your Future Dreams

The past held clues as to your future direction in the previous chapters, and the same applies here with money. The past will hold the snapshots that might stop you from being willing to move in your new direction with ease. If you have a financial blemish on your record, like bankruptcy or a failed business, or if you grew up with some resolution not to repeat your parents' financial past, you may need some soul-searching and forgiveness before attempting your crossover to something new. Money is the last hurdle to overcome.

Think back to when you got off track with money, either literally or figuratively. Literally means exactly when you started to falter with money—not doing well with it, never having enough, and often finding yourself in debt or in crisis mode. By figuratively, I mean that you are basically OK financially, but that it is not an easy topic for you. If you have any behavior around money that you are not proud of, find the start of it. It may just be the spot where you went off track.

An early mentor of mine had started his coaching practice after closing down a business that he struggled with for years until he finally had to declare bankruptcy. He talked about the shame he felt about the situation, and revealed that his life began to turn around only when he finally started to speak more freely about it and drop the shame. He felt better physically and emotionally when he was honest about it, as opposed to when he tried to sweeten the truth or shape it to avoid embarrassing himself in front of colleagues, friends, and clients. It was denying the truth that got his business to the point of bankruptcy. Examining those times when he went into denial and why allowed him to forgive himself and begin to move on. He now lives by a golf course with a successful practice that he attends to between rounds of golf.

In my own life, I can identify one of the times when I got off track with my "who" around money. I remember being a kid and going out for dinner every Sunday night. And every Sunday night when we returned home, my father would swear that it was the last time we were doing that because it cost too much money, only to take us out again the very next Sunday. As a result of this mixed message, I felt guilty that we went out, so I wouldn't ask to order anything other than what my father chose for us. To this day, when I look at a restaurant menu I have to remember that I am not nine years old and I can order whatever I want.

I hate to admit it, but I have even adopted my father's momentary panics about money. For me, it's more about larger purchases. Every time I spend a lot of money at once, even if it is not frivolous in the least, I get scared that we must go on an austerity budget immediately. I come home and announce that we are cutting back right away. I'd go so far as to say I was "bad" for spending. I learned this behavior early on. In some ways it served me, because it was that fear that helped me become a great saver and allowed me to buy my first home with the one-dollar bills from waitressing that I had stuffed into a safe-deposit box over the years. (If I had only known about investing then!) Later, however, I found it to be a source of unnecessary pain and a bad habit. I've become very conscious that I am not "bad" (or poor), and I stop myself before I say it now, but at one time it propelled me into emotional roller coasters that stretched from confidence to fear.

I call these untruths "money bugaboos." They are the lies we tell ourselves that render money powerless to perform its positive function in our lives. Again, they are beliefs so embedded in the fabric of our lives that they appear to be truths, but really are the hidden obstacles to being at ease and in good stead with the place money has in our life.

What's your bugaboo? Let's name it so we can minimize its power over you and reduce its ability to stop you from moving in your new direction.

> ### Exercise: *What's Your "Bugaboo"?*

Take into account the things you discovered about yourself and money in the previous exercise in this chapter. Use the chart below to help you assess the assumptions you make about money that get in the way of your happiness and to help you determine how to get around those obstacles.

Assumption About Money	Source	Truth About Money	Action to Correct Its Effect
There isn't enough money	Growing up in a frugal household	I make plenty to support myself and then some	Recognize the lie; stop saying it, even if I think it
I'm bad with money	I never let anyone help me because I want to be independent of my family	I need help	Ask some friends to teach me; find an adviser I trust
Spending is bad	When I asked for things when I was young, I was told I was greedy	I am responsible and can splurge once in a while	Stop torturing myself; enjoy what I have

(Continued)

Exercise (*Continued*)

Assumption About Money	Source	Truth About Money	Action to Correct Its Effect
I can't make it on my own	A childhood of poverty, always counting on others to take care of me	I have managed to budget and be responsible with what I have	Find people who can be examples; surround myself with cheerleaders; make a plan to be my own cheerleader

Barry, our MIT and Harvard grad from Chapter Four, shared his money bugaboo with me. Having grown up providing for himself since age fifteen, he made his first million before he was thirty, and he lived in fear that every dollar he spent would be his last. Ironically, he didn't much worry about making a living when he was financing his new direction. He was investing in start-up costs for his new consulting business, paying for his home, and being generous with his money with friends. Suddenly, he realized he had to get serious about bringing in an income, because his funds were not going to last forever. The stock market of the early 2000s was making that painfully clear. To combat his fear that every dollar would be his last, he had to admit that it was just not true. Then we had to come up with a strategy for allowing him to get into action and make a change, and to be able to stop feeling as though he was bleeding financially. He decided on one year's time and $60,000 as the investment he would make in building his business. Declaring that he would not let his change take any longer than a year propelled him to take more serious action and helped put a cap on his panicky feelings, because he had put a cap on his spending.

As we did earlier in the book, but now specifically about money, move your fears by illuminating what could be possible if you neutralized your approach to money. Shed what you don't like about yourself in terms of your behavior around money by taking action. Money is there to serve you, not to hinder you. However, if money is loaded with baggage, it will be tougher to take with you as you shift directions. Really examine the baggage and make sure you leave it behind. Most of it is just not true. Any part that is true can usually be overcome by focus, attention, and effort. Life tends to reward you for taking responsibility for what you have and don't have. It's when you blame circumstances on money instead of taking responsibility that luck seems to elude you. Examining your money bugaboos is one way to step up to the plate. Eliminating the imaginary problems leaves room for tackling the real ones, and that is a much more attractive *who* than being someone who blames everything around him for his plight or who spins her wheels by buying into her self-made lies.

When a Change Means Less Money

If your possible new direction would mean less money for you, your resolve may be tested. Will you ignore your Life Blueprint because of money? *Do What You Love, the Money Will Follow* is a popular book and saying, but you may have trouble believing it. That's reasonable. It's unseen, unproven, unknown. And the unknown is much scarier than staying with what's not working.

Start-up time, a gap in employment, a recovery or rest period, a divorce, time spent as a single earner or single parent, taking less pay to start in a new field—all are scenarios that can occur, but they are not necessarily permanent states. They can change and improve once you are on the other side. It's like a trapeze artist who can only get to the second swinging bar by letting go of the first one. It's scary as hell, but you can't make up the financial gap until you are in the new situation long enough to settle in and improve on it. Worrying won't do it, and you'll only grow more miserable as you wait. The key is to plan for the time you are airborne and on your way to grabbing that second bar.

There are many ways to create a safety net. Lori and Nick had been mulling a possible change for their life for a while, but were feeling stuck because Lori was the primary earner and she had no idea as to what else she would do. She made a handsome six-figure income as a television commercial talent, but she was at her wit's end with the unpredictability and fickleness of her industry and wanted to quit. She worried about replacing her income, but she knew she had to move on. Without a clear picture of what she was headed for, Lori and Nick decided that they needed to create a situation in which they had savings and time for Lori to figure out what was next. They knew that they could not afford to do that with the monthly nut they had to meet. Their two children were six years old and eighteen months old, so they felt the change would not be too jarring for them if they did something soon.

In a moment of brilliance, they realized that their prime New Jersey property and home was the best asset they had. They had family across the country in much more sane and financially reasonable places to live, so they decided they would move, make a profit on their home in the sizzling home market they were experiencing, and take their time to make new things happen for Lori. Nick knew he could find work in his old hometown, and Lori could work in a smaller market, doing commercials, and be a big fish in a small pond. Once the idea struck, they moved at lightning speed and did indeed score big on the sale of their home.

Lori and Nick built a cushion of time and money to foster an environment in which the changes could occur without pressure. If you already know which direction you are headed, it may even be easier to predict how long you'll be in limbo, planning for some kind of gap or realizing you'll be making a permanent financial change, and prepare for it.

Molly and Allan were another couple that financed their change in a similar way. Molly owned her own business but wanted to scale back so she could spend more time with her four children, and Allan had a corporate job but really longed to have his own business. They knew their "nexts," but they did not know how to finance them. They were caught in a cycle of believing they could afford a change if they worked harder and banked a little more. The problem was that their house was a huge financial burden that they could not seem to get ahead of. It took a lot of agonizing for them to finally decide to sell their house and move to a cheaper one a couple miles down the road. They experienced what I considered to be unnecessary shame about the move, but in the end, it was the best move they could have made. They had an instant savings account from the profit of their sale and significantly lower expenses to make every month. They both moved on to their "nexts."

I can appreciate what my clients go through. When I made up my mind that it was time to stop being a waitress (I became terrified upon discovering I had been doing that job almost longer than anything else in my short life) and start my entry into the training industry, it was like breaking myself of an addiction. I loved the cash, and I loved having the semblance of stability that a job gave me. However, I had gotten to the point where I had to make a choice and a leap of faith. I was not sure whether I would leave acting at that point, but I knew I had to leave my waitressing job and replace it with something that allowed me to like myself again.

I am often asked, especially by women, if my husband financed my gap between careers. That assumption makes me crazy, because the answer is *no!* At the time, my fiancé (now husband) had less money than I did. He was a broke actor, and I was a frugal one. My expenses were relatively low at the time, so what I did do was give myself an ultimatum. I took $10,000 out of my savings (remember, it was the 80s and I had a rent stabilized apartment in NYC, and I was *frugal*) and gave myself six months. Whichever ran out first, time or money, would determine when I needed to go back to waitressing or some other part-time job to get me by as I built my coaching and training business. I had six months to hustle, and hustle I did. I never went back to waitressing. I supplemented coaching with related work, such as presentation skill training or teaching English to executives, but I never needed a regular job again. But if I had not let go of waitressing, who knows if I would have ever really built my business to a sustainable level. It would have been too easy to stay trapped by the money. Once I was making my income from my coaching practice, I did some soul searching about acting and saw it was time to leave that, too.

Every life change needs time to gain speed and momentum, and, as I described with the metaphor of the trapeze artist, most of us will need to prepare for some time when we will be between successes. With your assessment of what you have and what you spend, now is the time to start getting creative about financing your change. If your change will not require this step, move on to the next chapter. The rest of us will be right here, using our creativity and resourcefulness to make the change work.

Investing in Yourself

The common thread you may have noticed in these last few stories is that the people in them all decided to invest in themselves. Whether it was time or money or both, they started to put some parameters around their transition. This is a critical step and one that will make change feel less scary. Just like a budget, you want to set up a structure to create from. When we set a period of time or an amount of money as the boundaries to a change, it helps us take very different action than if we just put out an ungrounded wish for the change to occur. A goal that helps us move along our path must be time-bound and measurable. We've avoided being linear and using logic through most of this process so far, but now we are going to put this very human strength of ours back into play to make the transition a reality. We perform better when we have a clear direction with a measurable checkpoint that allows us to monitor our progress.

> ### ▶ Exercise: *Investing in Yourself*
>
> Take pen to paper and explore what you can afford to invest in yourself. Pick a financial target and pick a time target, like my $10,000 or six months, or Barry's one year and $60,000. It's OK to have one or the other (time or money) or both. In other words, declare a deadline. For example, you might declare that you will take two years to transition to your new direction. Or you may decide to invest $10,000 in your training and one year to make a change. Remember, if you don't have money to invest, that is OK. We'll cover your options later in this chapter.

Charlie was an assistant director of television shows who had been in the industry for years and was now trying to start his own consulting business. He had some savings, and he occasionally took some directing work to keep the coffers full. He was very uncomfortable not having an income, and he had not really planned for the gap in employment before he pursued his new direction. When he came to me, he wanted to work to increase his business. One day when he was lamenting about what felt like financial hemorrhaging, I asked him if he could afford to make an investment in himself. He was silent for a moment as he thought about it.

"I never looked at it that way," he said.

On the spot, his perspective shifted, and instead of looking at his situation as an irresponsible rape and pillage of his savings, he decided on a time frame and a financial figure as an investment in himself he was comfortable with. In Charlie's case, the time he gave himself allowed him to recognize that being in a sole proprietorship and working alone was not the best way for him to go. He then began looking for opportunities to pursue his new skill set within an established business. But it was his ability to stop the fear by putting parameters on his investment that allowed him clarity and resolution.

It is really hard to have clear judgment or even be in touch with what feels right if you are in money panic, but having a time and money investment in yourself allows you the space to let life take its course. When you are not desperate, scared, or trying to push an outcome, the answers, and often luck, come more easily.

Moonlighting

Now, for those of you who have been waiting to shout: "But what if I don't have any assets to sell, or savings or investments to cash in on?" Can you still have your "it," your "next"? Yes! (What did you think I was going to say?)

Although I took a leap by making a complete break, I am a big advocate of moonlighting and using a conservative plan to cross over to something new. Moonlighting is a great bridge to a new future. There are very few people who will drop one thing entirely without some indication that the second thing will work out. In my case, I had savings and easy access to another job as plans B and C, so I felt I could afford to take the total risk of leaving one thing and having a gap before I got to the other. I was young, not yet married, no kids. Most of you will be carrying more on your shoulders, and you'll have to make the very personal decision as to whether you will make a complete break or cross over more slowly.

Moving slowly can have its advantages, too. Ralph owned a reputable advertising firm but had started to grow bored and wasn't sure what to do next. What became clear was that he wanted to start doing paid public speaking as a way to supplement his income with something that would make work exciting again for him. He had spoken without charging a fee whenever given the chance, but he wanted to make a go of it as a professional. He could not take time off from his current business, and he was the sole earner for a family of four. It did not take him long to get up the courage to ask for money when he was asked to speak. No one said no, and he kept raising his fee until he had a nice supplemental income coming in, at which time he could make a choice whether to go for it full-time or not.

One of my dear colleagues, Madeleine Homan, a mother of two and coauthor of *Leverage Your Best, Ditch the Rest,* wanted to be a corporate muckety-muck after years of consulting with artists and creative geniuses in her own business, advising them on how to become more successful. She moonlighted in someone else's company as a consultant and coach to get her experience working with the level of people she wanted to work with. As luck would have it, an opportunity arose to become crucial to a project within a bigger company, which eventually yielded a full-time executive position for her. She closed her business and made her transition into something different without having to invest any money.

It also pays to be proactive. An older client of mine was worried about retirement being five or so years away, knowing she would not be ready to stop working altogether but having no idea what else she would do. She had taken advantage of tuition reimbursement at her company to get a master's degree in library sciences. She wasn't really sure why, but it sounded interesting. She completed her degree, and even took a sporadic weekend job at a local library. As it turned out, she was let go from her company shortly before her official retirement would have come up. She left with a great severance package, retirement benefits, and health insurance, and after a short recovery period, she started working in a couple libraries and loved it—again, without investing any of her own money in the transition.

Sometimes it means getting started and watching for the right opportunity. Paul was a high-level human resources executive who felt the time had come to do something that would make him happy. He had dabbled for a long time with alternative healing methodologies (such as massage, acupuncture, and Reiki), first for his own well-being and then as an area of interest he began to toy with as a future career. With a family to support, he weighed his options carefully and then took advantage of his company's restructuring and negotiated a healthy package in order to make his exit. He applied for government money through his unemployment office to retrain as a massage therapist. He completed his training and has successfully built a clientele.

If moonlighting turns out to be your way to go, there will come a time as you do something on the side that the frustration of not having full days to devote to your new direction will start to get to you. That is a clear sign that it may be time to take the leap of faith. It is the breaking point when you can't afford not to devote your full attention to it. And it's hopefully the time you needed to create the financial cushion to give it its due. Any money made moonlighting would be put to good use as savings that can tide you over when the time comes to take the leap.

Notice that it is a leap of faith and not a leap of certainty, so there is no right time or right way to do it. It is like finding the right sweetheart to commit to. When you know, you know. The decision to take a leap of faith works the same way. You'll know when you know. It must feel right, albeit a little scary. It cannot feel contrived, like you are manipulating an outcome. Just experience the exhilarating (and alternating) fear and joy. They can feel awfully close!

Cutting Those Expenses

Whether you are preparing for a gap because of a change in marital status, relocating, or beginning the crossovers we've explored above, it makes sense to examine where you can cut back financially to make it a more comfortable ride. Again, a lot of this is common sense, and you don't need me to spell it out for you, so I will focus here on some of the less obvious ways to stretch your money.

In his book titled *Second Acts*, Stephen Pollan, a longtime lawyer and financial life adviser, says it well when he recommends that you "save dollars and not pennies." What he means, and what I subscribe to, is that there is little sense in making yourself crazy by cutting back in little ways that make you feel deprived. It is more significant to look for places to save a hundred dollars or more, so your cuts can really count toward reducing your expenses. For example, reducing your insurance costs by a few hundred dollars per year will take you further than giving up your daily coffee on the run.

However, if it makes you feel good to know that you are saving pennies, too, then by all means, go for it. Every bit helps.

Home-Related Ideas

➤ The boon of the bad economy we have been facing at this writing is the low interest rates on lending. Refinancing your home at the lowest rates in decades can allow for significant savings in your budget. You may be able to save even more money if you apply for a long-term adjustable-rate mortgage. You take a risk that interest rates will climb during the life of your loan, but in the short term, you can get your payments down lower. In the longer term, if cash flow improves, you can save thousands of dollars over the life of the loan by paying extra each month. It does not take much overpaying to make the savings add up.

➤ We talked about relocating to a less expensive place earlier in this chapter. This belongs on the list here as well.

➤ If you have not experienced any loss of employment, and can show the bank you are stable, consider getting a home-equity line of credit. The interest rates are very low, you don't owe anything unless you write checks from it, and if you use it for emergencies only, it is a lot cheaper than using credit cards if you get in a bind.

➤ Consider increasing the deductible on your homeowner's insurance. You really need protection from major loss or damage, not the minor stuff, so upping your deductible could make a significant contribution to your savings. You could save a couple hundred dollars annually on your policy without a lot of risk.

➤ Appeal your property-tax assessment. Most towns have a process for this. Ask at your municipal building. You will have to weigh the pros and cons of moving ahead after you get the initial comparisons to other properties in your area, because sometimes you are waking a sleeping dragon only to find you appealed your tax rate and they found they weren't charging you enough! If it is in your best interest to contest your tax assessment, it could save you thousands over the years.

Cars

➤ Again, increasing your deductible on your car insurance can save you money in the long term.

➤ If you drive a very old car or have an old car you keep on hand, you may want to revisit the insurance on it. If the car is not worth much, it could pay to get rid of your collision insurance, because that could save you a substantial amount on your monthly bill. If it costs more to insure it for collision than it does to replace it, you have your answer.

➤ Buying outright vs. leasing is always an interesting debate. I would suggest looking at it in terms of the long term vs. the short term and where you require the most savings. Leases are an attractive and seemingly affordable way to have the car you most want. However, you will always have a car payment and will have to come up with up-front cash every two or three years if you don't buy the car when the lease is up. However, since leasing allows you to really only buy part of a car's life, you have a smaller up-front fee. Buying a car means having the cash outright or taking a loan to finance it. It is probably best to lease a preowned vehicle. That is where you will save the most money.

Services

➤ If you have an expertise or own something that people need (like a snowblower!), you may be able to barter for the things you need.

➤ If there is a service you receive that you can recruit others to receive, you may be able to work out a discount from a provider for bringing in new customers.

➤ Cut back by getting a haircut, manicure, or other service once every six weeks instead of every four weeks, or once every ten days instead of once a week, and save over the course of the year.

➤ Swap babysitting duties with friends, and save both families a lot of money.

Education

➤ If you haven't already taken advantage of the newer 529 college savings plans, please do. Ask your financial adviser. These plans allow you to earmark money for education and put it away tax-free.

➤ Many schools will make deals in exchange for prepayment. This is very speculative on your part, but could help save down the line.

Life Insurance

➤ Review your life insurance policies based on your new needs and situation. Many policies have provisions to suspend some payments if you have a cash-value policy.

Consumer Credit

➤ You want to eliminate your credit card debt as much as possible. If you do take a home equity line of credit, it may behoove you to pay off the credit cards, because you will be repaying the bank at significantly lower rates than the cards charge you.

➤ This would also be a good time to review all your credit cards and their interest rates. It is so easy to sign up for a card at a low rate and not be aware of when the interest rate gets raised on you. Wipe out all high-interest credit card rates by consolidating, transferring, or considering the option above.

These are just a few ideas about how to cut costs to make your transition more comfortable. Hopefully, they are ideas you might not have considered. I'm relying on you for common sense and your own comfort level for the simpler, more penny-related cuts you may want to make.

I'd like happiness to be your bottom line. If you really worked through this chapter, you should have overcome your last logical resistance to making a change. Now you only have to manage the day in, day out fear of being in flight and making your life take off. That's the fun part!

> ## Questions to Ponder

What was most startling about looking at my money situation?

What was most exciting about looking at my money situation?

What do I like/dislike about who I am in terms of money?

What is my money bugaboo?

Who would I like to be in terms of money?

What do I need to do financially to move in a new direction?

What, specifically, am I willing to do to make an investment in myself and my transition?

What am I willing to sacrifice to get there?

What did I learn about myself in this chapter?

Life Often Does Imitate Art: Write Your Own Fiction

Why shouldn't truth be stranger than fiction? Fiction, after all, has to make sense.
— MARK TWAIN

If money has not stopped you, you're doing great. And you might be one of the people who wonders, "But how do I get *there* from *here?*" That's our next step. Your research project (which may still be ongoing at this point) probably began to reveal some ways to get there, but in this chapter we will be jogging your mind to think outside of the box. There's always a way to get "there," even if it does not register with you now. The key to uncovering the ways (there are likely to be many more than one) is to knock them from your noggin. Using the creative side of the brain will start to move you into seeing what is possible and start germinating the seeds that will grow into opportunities.

▶ **Exercise:** *Write Your Fiction*

Take pen to paper again, but this time, put on your best novelist's hat. Write five different and distinct scenarios that are possible ways you can get from where you are to where you'd like to be. Your fiction can be close to your real life, or it can be outrageous. Whatever occurs to you as a joyful way to have your possibility become a reality is fair game.

If you are reading ahead here without clarity on your "it," then use finding "it" as the goal you are writing your fiction about. In that case, the five scenarios will be about how you found "it." If you get terribly stuck, engage a friend to help you come up with the scenarios. Go for no less than five.

Here is an example from a client whose "it" was to find her next incarnation as a human resources specialist:

I am out in Las Vegas, playing blackjack. I am killing them at the table and just can't lose. I have a strategy and a plan — that's why. A high-level executive from a huge corporation who has been observing my play for the last hour or so sits down next to me and strikes up a conversation. He says, "I noticed your play, and you are very strategic and consistent, and you take just the right amount of risk. The game, like life, is riddled with luck. However, the way you have approached your game takes a lot of the luck out of the equation . . . which I like to see. How about I give you $20,000, and let's see what you can do with it. If you lose it, no biggie, and we will part ways. If you

> double it, I will give you half and hire you to come
> work for me, and you will make it big one day." I
> doubled his money in one hour, and he hired me on
> the spot to run his Chicago office.

Out of the Ridiculous
May Come the Sublime

As you saw in the last example, the scenarios can be pretty far-
fetched, but their wisdom may be very real indeed. The Blackjack
Queen saw that her scenario emphasized the importance of having a strategy and a plan, and that how she played the game allowed her to take luck out of the equation. Although she did not
see this scenario as a motivator to get on a plane to Vegas, she did
feel as though it sent her a message. She needed to stop waiting
around for luck to find her, and if she really did want to move up
in her profession, she was going to have to come up with a strategy and a plan. The fictitious scenario gave her the "oomph" to
get her butt in gear.

Remember Janelle, from Chapter Four? She was the CPA
who volunteered with women's leadership groups but at first did
not see the connection between her volunteer work and a possible new direction for her life and career. At first, she had absolutely no clue what she might do next in her life. She was a
single mom and had practiced in her field for 25 years. She did
not feel as though there were many options out there. When I
first suggested to her that there might be a connection between
her current work and her volunteer work, she listened politely.

The second time I pointed it out was when I asked her to do

the exercise you just completed. She felt I was forcing the issue, and resisted looking at it as a possible new direction. I told her to appease me by doing the five scenarios that might get her from CPA to executive director or an officer at a nonprofit. She begrudgingly agreed. I would never want her to substitute her judgment for my own, but I also knew she needed to jog her mind if there was any chance of identifying a new "it." Logic was not cutting it.

When Janelle returned from doing the exercise, she was upbeat and hopeful. She hated to admit that something had clicked for her while doing the exercise, but she did eagerly share that she discovered through her fictitious scenarios that she indeed wanted to run some kind of project and have more contact with people in the process. She could not yet imagine any packages that fit this criteria, but in subsequent weeks, she rewrote her résumé to play up the direction she wished to go. Her scenarios also allowed her to see who she could benefit from visiting or interviewing to find out more. Making contact with those people started the ball rolling toward possible "nexts." It also reminded her of her passion for food, travel, and entertainment, and that those things were exciting options to research, too. Her creativity began to flow again. That is a very good sign of progress. If, like Janelle, you are still working things through, fiction can help you get out of the logical line of thinking that may be keeping you stuck.

Jon, who you met in Chapter Five, already had his "next" by this point. He was a branding expert who had gone out on his own a year prior to meeting me and was working in advertising agencies before that. His schooling and training were in architecture and design. He wanted to reconcile his lifelong love of animals and nature, and his newly discovered purpose of helping others experience the awe of nature. He was finally allowing himself to dream of making his living by being a nature guide or the owner of an adventure-travel company.

"How do I get there from here?" he wondered. His five fictional scenarios reflected ways that he might transition into new opportunities. His versions were long and colorful. I've paraphrased four of them here. They included:

➤ Kayaking in Alaska with a group. Jon became critical to keeping a less experienced kayaker from panicking in thirty-four-degree seawater. His demeanor was discussed back at camp, and the tour owner/guide approached Jon about joining his company. The guide saw Jon's design and branding expertise as a plus to his tour-leading potential, and a new venture was born.

➤ Camping with friends who were all amateur chefs yielded an innovation in cookware for lovers of outdoor sports. Jon was in Asia, producing the line, and was designing his sixth product. He began getting offers to develop innovative outdoor gear and test them by going on expeditions.

➤ Jon was standing 1,400 feet above the Hudson Valley with a young girl and her "big sister" (a sponsor and mentor assigned by Big Brother/Big Sister, Intl.). He was moved by their newfound awe of nature and the incredible view, and they struck up a conversation about a nonprofit group that introduces city people to outdoor activities. Jon expressed his interest in being part of such an organization, and the following Monday morning the woman recommended him for a job with the group.

➤ Jon was in Whistler, British Columbia, hanging by a rope from a rock face. As he paused to take some pictures from his vantage point, he considered an offer made by someone in the two-month outdoor leadership training program he was taking part in. The man who made the offer ran an outdoor magazine. He was just about to redesign the look of his publication, and upon learning that Jon had design skills and innovative ideas (he had noticed Jon's unique self-designed outdoor gear), he asked Jon to join him. Jon said he wasn't interested in a regular office job. The man said he wanted Jon to be his art director, which would not only include designing the physical look of the magazine, he would also be required to join all expeditions and photo shoots, and direct and style them as well.

Before we get too carried away with our fiction-writing prowess, it might be useful to know how fiction helps you form the future. The act of writing and reading your fiction trains your intellect, primes your intuition, and informs your subconscious in such a way that you begin to notice the opportunities that can float you to your desired outcome. It causes you to become a bit of a transmitter, like a broadcast tower. You are sending out a signal and receiving one at the same time. Writing fiction causes your brain to expand to new possibilities. It puts you in a state of anticipation and hope, which then allows you to open yourself to opportunities and symbolic encouragement that you may not have noticed before, even if it was right under your nose. You are also transmitting nonverbally that this is what you are up to, and synchronicity does occur.

It reminds me of when I bought my first car. As my husband and I transitioned from poor actors to start-up business owners, we bought a Ford Explorer. (I have since given up SUVs because of their gas mileage.) We were so excited to get this car, and suddenly we seemed to notice Explorers everywhere, although we had hardly noticed them before. Once our awareness was focused on one type of car, Explorers were all we seemed to see.

Similarly, your fiction will make you more aware of the opportunities that are already out there. It can also cause a ripple effect: giving you ideas, putting you into action, attracting opportunities, and training your world to respond in kind. Fiction helps you break through old thinking patterns and create a new logic that works for you. Writing and rereading your fiction often allows it to get into your cells and your muscle memory. When you combine this mental exercise with action, you increase your chances of making your Life Blueprint's mandate even clearer.

Keep these fiction exercises (and the one we will do later in this chapter) close at hand and read them often. Just as you do when you read a novel, you will form pictures in your mind. With a novel, you might see in your mind's eye what the characters look like, what the places and things that are described look like, and you essentially begin to play a movie in your mind. When you read your own fiction, you are doing the same thing and programming your mind as you go. The effect is similar to athletes using visualization to improve their performance. They see it in their mind's eye, as a way to train themselves and their muscles to perform. You will be seeing the fiction in your mind's eye, as a way to absorb it into your psyche and realize that anything is possible.

In case you were wondering, your fictitious scenarios may not be carried out, and probably won't reflect the exact way that things will go down. They are merely exchanges between your reality and your imagination, which multiply the possibilities. You may find that some pieces of your fiction come true. You may find that a great idea about how to pursue your direction comes from the scenarios, or they may just serve as entertaining vignettes that bring a smile to your face. No matter which they become, they will have served in expanding your awareness and training your mind to watch for opportunities.

Yeah, But . . .

Adele Sheely, a career counselor I once had the pleasure of sharing a workshop with, said: "The number of 'yeah, buts' is in direct correlation to the depth of your fear."

Are you a "yeah, but" person? Do you know any "yeah, but" people? You might have thought they were argumentative and maybe really smart, but what if all they were was afraid? Afraid of change, or afraid of entertaining anyone else's point of view. If we are indeed describing you, which are you afraid of?

This process has offered many, many opportunities for fear, your ego, and/or your inner critic to pop up with perfectly logical reasons that it is ridiculous to consider any kind of change. Writing your fiction will be another ripe opportunity for doubt and fear to pop up. It's perfectly normal, so please don't judge yourself. If you are not experiencing any doubt, but are just excited about it all, hold on, because we will be addressing that in a moment. If you are feeling somewhat resistant, just keep going, even if you think it's only to go through the motions. If you are not sure if you are being resistant, but sure that your common sense is kicking in to save you from yourself, let me spell out some examples that might address your issues and calm your fears.

Austin had recently moved his entire family from Kansas to Seattle for a job opportunity. He had never left his hometown, and had uprooted his family from all their friends and extended family. Barely two years after moving, another even better opportunity came up within the company, but it meant a move to Chicago. Austin really wanted the job, but his "yeah, but" had to do with his kids. "Yeah, but what about the kids? I can't uproot them again!"

Austin had written five fictitious scenarios that included, among other things, commuting, moving everyone to much delight, staying, and getting other opportunities. The one that kept resonating with him was the scenario in which everyone moved happily. Without even talking to his wife and kids, he was letting the "yeah, but" be so definitive that he hadn't even thought of asking them what they thought. With a big nudge, he did so, and after the initial shock, the family became excited about the possible move. The kids had always wanted to see a big city like Chicago. His wife was excited about the schools she had heard about for the kids. They even liked the idea of experiencing winters like they never had before.

Austin was shocked. This was not what he had expected. And to think he almost let the "yeah, but" stop him! It was *his* fear, not necessarily his family's, that was stopping him. This illustrates the sophistication of fear. It knows how to spin things just right, so the fear sounds so logical and reasonable.

Another common "yeah, but" and point of contention for people is the whole issue of not being "ready." "I'm not ready to date." "I'm not ready to make a change." "I'm not ready to go for the dream." Whichever version has crossed your lips or your ears as you listened to someone else, I have no doubt that you know what I mean.

Lydia was one of those people who was not ready. She had found that her "it" was teaching. She had already earned her certificate, after having completed the necessary courses and requirements. Her fiction established her as a popular teacher through many different venues and scenarios. In reality, she found herself looking at the want ads and applying for jobs outside of teaching. She was behaving as if she had not taken all the steps to enter her new chosen field. She still felt she needed to do other things first to prove she was ready. Her "yeah, but" was that no one would hire her because she hadn't gotten her bachelor's degree in education or childhood development or something that proved her ability to work with children as a teacher. She didn't feel ready. She felt she needed to *know* more.

When she was made aware that her "yeah, but" was a reflection of being afraid, she agreed to slowly take the steps to secure her place in her new profession. After a couple months, she did indeed get a teaching job, and saw many of her fictitious scenarios as a popular teacher come to be.

One of my favorite lines from a very silly movie speaks to this topic very well. In *Pee Wee's Big Adventure*, Pee Wee says to his new friend, the waitress, after she just finished describing her life's dream to him and then followed it with a huge sigh and a "but . . .": "Everyone I know has a big *but*."

What's yours?

> **Exercise:** *Yeah, but . . .*

Take a moment to write down your "yeah, but," if indeed one has cropped up for you. In writing, work your way through it by recognizing it as fear. Record what it is you are really afraid of, and take action or have the discussions needed to help you get past it. Conquering this one should help keeping future "yeah, but" attacks at bay.

Hobby by Emergency

If the invitation to write fiction about your future direction has stumped you, or you've found it really difficult to let the ideas flow, I've got a special assignment for you. Don't judge yourself or get all nuts about it, but I do have news for you, too. You're desensitized. You are cut off from your senses. You need a break. You need to get back into your body and your senses. You need a hobby and you need one now.

I am completely serious. If this last exercise was hard for you, I need you to add a couple of weeks to this process by choosing an activity that will get you back to *feeling* and therefore opening up your ability to use your imagination. It will only take a couple of weeks to turn your senses back on, but you must, *must* do this for the program to work for you.

Here are some ideas:

Running	Pottery
Beading	Yoga
Knitting	Painting
Dancing	Woodworking
Building with your hands	Practicing a musical instrument

You'll want to choose something that either involves working with your hands or something that engages the whole body. Either one will work for our purposes. It may be something that came up as an interrupted dream from your life story in Chapter Four. If you have any doubt that this can work, let me tell you a couple of remarkable stories about what a difference a hobby (even as a last resort) can make.

Ellen had been struggling for several years to decide what course her working life should take. She had worked with one of the coaches on my team for a long time and then studied with me, and she also took part in our *Now What?* public program. When we got to the fiction portion of the process, Ellen's five outrageously fictitious scenarios went something like this:

1. I could get a new job
2. I could make a lateral move in my company
3. I could talk to contacts about a job with them
4. I could retrain for another career
5. I could switch departments where I now work

Yikes! A hobby was in order immediately! Ellen's life juice, her imagination, and her ability to move her life forward were in danger of becoming extinct. Ellen chose to get back on her bike, and committed to cycling four or five times a week. It only took two weeks to see a remarkable change in her. She had renewed energy, was much less numb to her own feelings and desires, and was able to have some clarity about what was holding her back. She got out of being completely stuck and blind to opportunity. She was hopeful for the first time in a long time.

Ellen was able to see and articulate that she was white-knuckling and holding on to what she perceived as financial security from her job. She did not trust any of her inklings and ideas as to what might be next nor was she honoring any of the things she knew she wanted, because she had worried herself into a corner. She feared not being able to make money in any way other than what she was doing now. It was a relief for Ellen to be able to put words and feelings to her fears instead of feeling hopelessly stuck. After two weeks, she was not yet able to create outrageous fiction, but she had succeeded in letting some long-held truths and desires come through. Some ideas that popped up included doing something with animals, working around beautiful objects, working around the water, and finding a career where she could work and live anywhere she wanted to. This was huge progress. These were tangible things that rang true when she spoke about them, and they were full of life as compared to her previous musings (or lack thereof). Once there was life back in her and she was more in touch, we were able to go on with the program.

Vanessa is another example of how hobby-by-emergency can work, and her story opens up all kinds of possibilities. Vanessa chose beading as her hobby. She found a local bead shop that sold beautiful, exotic beads from all over the world. The shop owner also offered beading classes on site, so Vanessa pushed beyond her comfort zone to join the group as a way to commit to her hobby. What ensued was very interesting.

Vanessa was in her fifties and lamented that in her entire life she had never been able to get a handle on what she wanted. Sure, she could decipher her feelings enough to be gainfully employed, own a home, and go about her daily life, but when it came to holding a vision of what she wanted her life to look like or what dreams she held, she was cut off—desensitized. Working through things leading up to this fiction-writing chapter, Vanessa had been able to identify a few wishes. She would love to find a way to afford to travel the world, and she hoped that she could somehow have art or some of the finer things in life at her disposal. How to bring those ideas into reality or find a connection in her current life to those desires left her guessing and therefore putting them into the fantasy category. In other words, they had become something she felt she could do nothing about.

Back to the bead shop, and we find Vanessa beginning to really enjoy her new hobby. The beads are just works of art in themselves, the people are nice, and Vanessa's designs surprise her. She had a flair for putting the elements together to create jewelry that merited attention. Again, as in Ellen's case, it was only a matter of a couple of weeks before Vanessa's *feeling* capacity began to grow. With feeling came excitement and wonder, and with them came a curiosity about what she was doing that led her to befriend the bead store owner. In asking him all sorts of questions about his work, Vanessa found that the owner traveled all over the world buying beautiful beads for his store, and that he was considering selling the business in a couple of years.

Do you see what I see? Beads are a thing of beauty, and some would even say they are art. World travel. A business based on both those things. Did Vanessa buy his business? Well, it's too early to tell, but she did feel she wanted to build a relationship with the owner and she had her dreaming mechanism turned back on. She could see how her inklings could become a reality, this way or some other way. After just a couple of weeks of hobby-by-emergency work, she had a renewed sense of self, energy, vision, and in her words: "I am able to say what I want for the first time in my adult life! *That* is nothing short of a miracle."

Here's another one. Lynn felt terribly stuck although she was well on her way to starting her own ministry. She was tripping herself up with all kinds of self-imposed limits every step of the way. "Analysis paralysis" (doing nothing because one has worried or mentally stacked the deck against themselves) was setting in and she needed to be knocked out of it. Hobby by emergency was assigned.

Lynn decided to make glass designs that were a form of stained glass work. She remembered spending hours in church every Sunday staring at the beautiful stained glass windows and, as an adult, visiting beautiful churches with glasswork around the world. When she decided on glasswork, she took to it right away and got her energy back almost instantly. She was so enthused by the hobby that she entered her very first piece in a contest and won first place. This was so encouraging that she started to divide her attention between growing her ministry and doing her artwork, and has, in fact, launched a side business for her art. Her hobby gave her back her life: her focus, her energy, her dreaming mechanism, and her love for life.

If you had trouble writing your fiction, please take on this assignment and take on the antidote to desensitization. If you wrote your outrageous fiction without much trouble, you can carry on from here without a hobby break, but I hope you can see where this might serve you too as you go on your way. And remember, although the examples are about three women, men succeed with this as well.

The Free Fall

Imagine that you've talked yourself into diving out of a plane to prove that you can do anything. You are standing at the edge where the physical matter of the airplane ends and the mind-bending vastness of sky begins. The wind is forcing your eyes to close as you try to keep your balance 15,000 feet above the ground. You are tethered to your instructor for your first jump ever. The command has been given to go, and you close your eyes and jump! You have taken the free fall.

Moving your life in a new direction often feels like a free fall, and that is the term I use to encourage people who share that they are about to start something new. You are taking a free fall—an act of trust that you feel reasonably sure will result in a positive outcome, but that feels incredibly exhilarating and scary at the same time.

We talked briefly about leaps of faith and when to take them, but a free fall is more immediate and can happen several times in the course of making a change. A free fall is the feeling of being suspended in a state where time seems to stand still long enough for you to question what you are doing while at the same time knowing that it is exactly the right thing to do. It's a feeling that might be visited several times a day or only occasionally (and maybe never), but it's positive, not something to fear. If for a moment you thought it might feel like a panic attack, don't worry—it doesn't. It's like the feeling you may have experienced when your first love showed that he/she was as interested in you as you were in him or her: a breathless excitement filled with wonder and awe, peppered with the fear of the unknown and a disbelief that it was happening. I never heard it put as well as one client recently put it: "I am not afraid, and that should scare me, but it doesn't!" That's the free fall—so many familiar emotions scrambled out of logical order.

> ### ▸ Exercise: *Free-Fall Fiction*
>
> Your next work of fiction will be in timeline form. In my experience, most transitions take between one and two years to complete. Choose which time frame resonates with you, and start writing your story accordingly.
>
> *(Continued)*

Exercise (Continued)

If you think it will take one year to settle into your new situation, write about what life will look like one year from now, personally and professionally. Next, write about the previous six months, and all the action that had to be taken to get you to that one-year mark. Last, write about the three months that came before the six-month mark. What did you have to do to reach your six-month mark?

Similarly, if you are aiming for a two-year transition, write about your life two years from now, one year from now, and six months from now.

Be sure to first start with the date that's furthest away, and write the rest of your fiction by backing up and describing what had to happen at that stage to yield the next stage.

After you complete the exercise above, take a look at the fiction you just wrote. It may reflect some of the elements of the five scenarios you did earlier; it may not.

I asked you to do this last exercise in reverse order for a reason. If I had asked you to first write about the most immediate steps to take, followed by the next ones, and the next ones, resulting in a year of action, your brain would go right into linear, logical thought. Doing it in the reverse order allows for creativity and tricks your brain into exploring more options. Now that we have the backward timeline, I would like you to use it to form a forward timeline. The steps at the three-month or six-month stage will now become your first benchmark, and should naturally reveal which actions you need to take. We will do a more complete action plan in the next chapter.

Sometimes your transition may take longer than you planned for and other times it will happen more quickly. Roxanne had known for ten years that she wanted to leave her marriage. She promised herself she would not take action until her children were headed to college, and that time was approaching. Although her relationship was strained, and both she and her husband knew their days as a couple were numbered, she still needed to make a transition mentally, emotionally, financially, and physically (that is, actually moving out).

In writing her free-fall fiction, she determined that she wanted to complete this transition in one year. Within a year, she wanted to be set up in her own place, be financially independent of her husband, and be happily pursuing her own interests. To do so, the six-month mark needed to show that the divorce was almost complete, that she had identified where she wanted to live, and that she knew what she could count on financially. (She had always worked, so she did not have to figure out how to make a living.) At the three-month mark, she needed to have been in contact with a divorce attorney, let her kids know what was going on, start identifying what she wanted to take with her, and allow herself to believe that this transition was really happening.

For Roxanne, the timeline made her steps so clear that she could not stand waiting any longer. Instead of making the transition in one year, she made it in seven months. Although she had planned to wait until her first child went to college to start any action, she felt she had to start right away. She contacted an attorney, hashed things out with her husband, told her kids, identified an area of town that she could afford to live in, and found the resolve within herself to make it all work.

Roxanne knew that she needed to make more money, even

though the divorce would provide some division of assets that she could count on. In addition to her full-time job, she found another related position for a few hours a month that would make up the difference for her financially. As for her kids, they took the news well, since they had sensed it coming anyway and were old enough to understand the basic idea that their parents would always love and respect each other, but would no longer be living together. In the end, she wondered why she had waited so long.

The backward timeline has proven effective in uncovering solutions where people thought they'd already exhausted their options. Stefan used his free-fall fiction to calculate how he would achieve his desire to have his successful entrepreneurship stop interfering with his family life. Within a year, he wanted to have manifested a way that he could travel less, manage his three distinct business interests, and have more days at home with his wife and kids. In order to have the family life he wanted, he would have to cut back on his work, something he was not willing to do. Deadlock? Not necessarily. By taking a crack at this fiction exercise, Stefan saw that he needed to physically move his business or his home (or both!) in order to bring them closer together, thus reducing his travel distance and giving him time to be more of a presence in his own home. Doing the exercise backward allowed him to see this. He had been trying to do it logically (and forward) for a few years to no satisfaction.

Weight loss is always a big change that people attempt to make, and although it's not my area of expertise, you may be curious to know how the backward timeline helped one of my clients break out of destructive eating habits. Caren was her name, and she dreaded any attempt at fitness or losing weight because she had made so many failed attempts. She had been considering finding a new line of work, and after doing the timeline exercise for her career, she decided to try it on her other goal.

In her fiction, she wrote that one year out, she was at her goal weight, wearing great clothes, feeling confident in her work, having her choice of friends and dates, and enjoying her life to the fullest. In her fictitious timeline, that meant that at the six-month mark she was well entrenched in an eating program and exercise regime and was doing it with a few other women, who kept one another on track. She also noted that by this point she had gotten rid of a third of the weight that she wanted to lose.

Her fictional three-month mark reflected that she had been out walking and ran into a woman with a group of supporters who kept her on track with her exercise and who invited Caren to join them. She had rid her house of all tempting foods, and she had rid her closet of any clothes that were too big or too small. She gave away the big ones and put the small ones in another room until they fit. Not having a daily reminder of how far she had to go was helpful for her.

Upon rereading her fiction, she felt different than she had at times when she tried to gather her resolve to "go healthy." She did not feel the dread, nor did she feel as though an eternity of deprivation stood in front of her. Instead, she felt energized and hopeful that this time would be different. She remarked that reading her fiction every day helped her visualize the outcome she was working toward and not feel tethered by the daily steps that could seem so negative. It was attainable because she could remember the big picture while the small steps were adding up to something. She could do that without it being overwhelming and stopping her.

She did not end up bumping into someone who invited her to be part of a support group, but her fiction writing gave her the idea to find one. Doing so was instrumental to her losing 30 pounds over the course of the next several months.

A New Logic

By now, I hope I have succeeded in demonstrating that logic, as you know it, is not necessarily helpful and that if you haven't already, it is time for you to redefine what is logical and what isn't. A new logic is in order; anything is possible. If you allow "anything is possible" to be your new logic, your linear action will be supported in a whole new way. It will be floated by that new belief and will not lead you astray. The following chapter will reveal even more amazing stories that will serve as evidence that anything is possible, but it is here that I want to see you adopt this tenet. Patti did.

Patti, who you'll remember as the woman who vowed to have more fun on her job and be more herself, said it so well: "Anything's possible. I feel like a kid again. You know how kids feel that they can be anything they want to be? That's how I feel. I can be anything I want to be!"

Patti was describing the exhilaration of the free fall. It is a high that will come and go, but if you can hold on to its message that anything is possible, you have succeeded at creating a new framework that will make achievement easier.

▶ **Questions to Ponder**

What parts of me, if any, are challenged or threatened as I write fiction about my life?

What is my current "yeah, but" that still holds me back?

What was the common thread, if any, to my fictitious scenarios?

What did I learn from the fiction I wrote?

What did I learn about myself in this chapter?

What has become undeniably clear as my first step?

Put Yourself in Opportunity's Way

> *You have to leave the city of your comfort*
> *and go into the wilderness of your intuition.*
> *What you'll discover will be wonderful.*
> *What you'll discover will be yourself.*
>
> —ALAN ALDA

You've prepared the landscape by doing the imaginary work, and now it is time to move entirely out of your sphere and put yourself in opportunity's way. A momentum has already been created. You may be seeing results as your research project leads you from conversation to conversation, and perhaps to real opportunities. Your fiction writing also may have prompted some movement in your life. In this chapter, you are going to increase the momentum and start moving into your new direction.

Chérie Carter-Scott, Ph.D., author of *If Life Is a Game, These Are the Rules*, says: "Want leads to choice, which leads to commitment. Should leads to decision, which leads to sacrifice." If there is any sense of sacrifice as you move forward, it would be a good idea to stop and look at what is left that is not genuinely you. If you are off course from your Life Blueprint, you'll feel like you *should* be doing this or that. I define "should" as "someone else said so," so if you are experiencing any of that, stop now and go back and dig for the truth about what *you* want. This process will only bloom for you if you have told the truth about who you are and what you want. There is still time to go back and do so.

If you are still feeling excited (terrified but curious is OK, too), then this is the time to make a commitment to yourself that you will see this direction through. "How do I know if this is really what I'm meant to be doing?" many a client or workshop participant has asked at this point, with a slight panic in their voice. As I tell them, and I now tell you, you don't have to decide if it's what you are meant to be doing. Life will decide that for you. All you have to do is make a commitment to keep going in that direction until it is clear that you are off course (which is not likely). When you're facing the right direction, all you need to do is walk.

It doesn't mean that your pursuit may not present challenges, but it does mean that you'll overcome them if your commitment is clear. You'll know if you made a mistake if your direction stops making you happy. If everything you do results in a dead end, you may have misread the signs. But again, by this point in the process, I'd say it's just fear that's causing your doubts, and it is highly unlikely that you've made a bad choice.

On the other hand, you might experience what Claire did. Claire, who you read about in Chapters One and Two, had been diligently working each stage of the process as you have when she began her research project. By making a few phone calls to learn about possibly crossing over into event planning, she opened up a flow of information and opportunities that overwhelmed her like a giant waterfall. She felt as though she was drowning, and she began to panic. Her contacts had other contacts for her, and one of them even wanted to put her in touch with a recruiter who could place her in a job. Claire got so freaked out that she wished there was a switch that she could use to turn off the deluge. She immediately questioned if this was really the direction she should be going in. She only meant to do research, not to make a change immediately, after all!

I reminded Claire that she could stop making phone calls and take things at her own pace, but that I interpreted the flow of information and opportunity as a clear sign that she was headed in the right direction. She still wanted to check out the other areas she was interested in and do more research, all of which was perfectly reasonable. She, in essence, needed to put a cap on the flow of things just as you would cap off a city fire hydrant that popped its top on a hot summer day. We both knew that the opportunities would still be there when she was ready. As it turned out, she took things at her own pace, gave herself permission to slow down, and then found that she really did want to pursue all the leads she had and make the transition to event planning. She just needed time to adjust to her good fortune.

Follow Your Nose

As you saw with Claire's story, one of your possible directions will take on a momentum of its own. It's probably the one you were most interested in anyway, but an accelerated momentum is a good sign that your Life Blueprint is kicking in. It doesn't require much on your part other than following your nose. What I mean by that is what I call "the Toucan Sam theory." Just as the colorful toucan from the box of Kellogg's Froot Loops cereal followed his nose to find his treasured bowl of breakfast fare, so will you follow your nose and your intuition to find the prize: your new life.

Intuition becomes an important part of the process. Your intuition has been working alongside you the whole time, whether you were aware of it or not, but now it will become a tool, one that will be worth the effort to use. The first and easiest step is just becoming open to it. All that really means is being a little quieter so you can hear your innermost inklings and ideas, and allow them to come to the surface. In essence, it just requires being open and listening to the whispers in the wind. Yes, even those that make you think you're crazy.

When I knew I had to leave waitressing and acting, and had no idea what else I could do, I was at a very vulnerable time in my life, when I was humbled and open to anything. I had no choice but to listen to a crazy notion that kept persistently showing up in my thoughts. I had this idea that I should call an old acquaintance from my acting days. I hardly knew him, and it had been years since I had seen him, but I remembered which town he lived in and looked him up through information. I felt like a fool as I got on the phone to call him, but this notion in my head kept repeating itself and, in fact, it spelled out that he had my next job or could lead me to my next career.

With my heart in my throat, I called his house, got him on the phone, and asked if he remembered me. He said yes. I went on to explain that I wasn't really sure why I was calling, but that I wanted to catch up with him. (I wasn't about to tell him that I was going crazy and that a voice was telling me to call him because he had the key to my future!) He politely entertained my rambling, and when he asked me what I was up to, I had to say that I felt I was done with this stage of my career, but I had no idea what else I would do.

The person from my past was Jay Perry, my first coach, who I have mentioned in some of my other work. He told me in that vulnerable, first conversation that he thought he could help me figure out what I wanted to do. I had never heard of coaching, but I did not care. All I knew was that there was an answer to my query and that there was someone who could help me find it. As it turned out, the crazy notion in my head was my intuition, dead-on in its direction. Through Jay, I founded my first training business, which in turn led to me becoming trained and credentialed as a professional coach, which led to the career you can read about at the end of this book. So my intuition was right: Jay would lead me to my next job or my next career.

So how do you know if you are tapping into your intuition? Intuition is quietly persistent. It just won't go away, and it will find different ways to infiltrate your awareness until you honor it. It will quietly nag you, or you will start to notice external things that remind you of what your intuition is trying to tell you. For example, friends might recommend a movie or a book that turns out to echo what you intuitively know you have to act on but have been trying to ignore. Or you'll bump into someone who does what you have been toying with doing, and you can't help but see it as a nudge to get your butt in gear and take action. Or you'll keep noticing billboards or commercials on TV that seem to be screaming a unique message to you, despite the product they are selling to the general public.

I remember driving along a busy highway once, on my way back from a meeting in New York City, when my attention was suddenly drawn to a giant billboard that showed an eighteen-wheeler truck trying to outrun a small, economy-size car. The slogan said: "Think Big!" At that moment, I had felt that the sign was there just for me. (Come to think of it, I never saw it again *anywhere*.) The meeting I was coming from had been disappointing, and I really could have been upset if I had not seen the billboard that seemed to hold a message just for me.

Intuitive knowing is your Life Blueprint emerging to the surface, begging you to follow it. It is the essential ingredient to expanding your awareness and consciousness on the road to a life that will satisfy you. This sixth sense wants your attention and is the basis for your evolution and growth. It is the magic of being human that only a few of us have come to trust. If you follow the clues it lays out, you will be amazed at how things can fall into place. James Redfield said it well in his book *Secrets of Shambhala*: "What we want instead [of a life reduced to survival] is a life filled with mysterious coincidences and sudden intuitions that allude to a special path for ourselves in this existence, to a particular pursuit of information and expertise—as though some intended destiny is pushing to emerge."

And yet, intuition can be tricky business, too. Without all the self-knowledge you've collected during this process, a barrage of ideas or intuitive leads can cause you to spin your wheels like a detective with too many clues to a crime to make any sense of them. Your intuition is there to be accessed and is a necessary part of bringing your new direction into being, but be sure to keep yourself grounded and not let it lead you astray. When it matches your purpose, your vision for yourself, your criteria for happiness, and your fiction, intuition acts as a marker, benchmark, and confirmation that you are on the right track. It can also lead you to your sweet spot where luck breaks through.

Luck, Coincidences, and Synchronicity

Jennifer came to me post-9/11 in a very desperate situation. Her business had dried up completely in the aftermath of the tragic events, and she wanted help getting the business back on its feet. Within one conversation with her, however, it was clear that a new direction for her life was calling her, but she was stubbornly hanging on to her sales training business because she could not reconcile the two directions. She revealed that she wanted to go back to school for a master's in divinity, but she could not imagine how she would pay for it. She barely had enough money to pay the rent, much less to make a living if she pursued that path.

Unwilling at first to explore the direction that her intuition was leading her in, Jenn insisted that our work together be about fixing and ramping up her current business. To me, it was obvious that there was no saving the current business until she explored what had shown up as an urgent roadblock, begging for her attention. Nonetheless, Jenn did not heed the call until it had become painfully obvious that she needed to take desperate measures to bring in an income.

"It's time to get a job," I said to her one day.

"Like what?" she replied.

"I don't know, maybe waitressing or bartending," I said seriously, at least for the moment.

Well, that was it. My words spurred her to admit that things were bad and that she had nothing to lose in exploring her options for going back to school. Within a few weeks, after having meetings at her two top choices of schools, she had an offer for a complete scholarship and subsidized housing from a distinguished seminary.

Jennifer gave up her office and her apartment, and prepared to move to her school. As she moved toward her new direction, the floodgates seemed to open and tens of thousands of dollars worth of sales training work poured into her business. She was going to attempt to do some of that work while she pursued her studies to relieve the months of debt she had accrued. She also found herself being offered an immediate summer position as an assistant pastor at her church, which she could do before her school session began. She was well on her way to her new direction.

Was it a coincidence that everything worked as it did? Was it luck? Well, I guess that depends on how you define luck. "Preparation meeting opportunity" is one popular definition. I define luck as the reward for taking responsibility for the truth. Because when you do, the universe seems to respond by moving in and taking over. Telling the truth releases pent-up energy that was invested in denying, disguising, or compensating for the truth. Then a vacuum is created for more energy to come in its place. That energy coming in brings movement in your life. Synchronicitous circumstances—or what you might call coincidences—begin to emerge.

Jennifer was not honoring her truest desire, becoming a minister. Who could blame her? She was a powerful businesswoman; how could she be thinking of throwing it all out the window? As you heard, she couldn't, so her business had to dry up completely before she would allow herself to really consider her innermost desire. Only when she took action toward the new direction did her business come back in full swing. She had also complained bitterly that she would not have the money to go back to school or to support two households to go and study somewhere. Well, synchronicity struck again when she was offered not one but two full scholarships, and housing to boot.

As I said earlier, you don't need to decide if you are on the right track; life will tell you. When you act on what is true for you, when it is coming from a place that is positive and it has the potential to serve others as well as make you a fuller contributor in the world, the tides seem to change in your favor. When you are after something for some of the wrong reasons (for example, competitive scheming, greed, ego gratification, or control) the battles seem longer and harder, but if that is your choice, know that results are still attainable.

Since I played with the definition of luck, let's also define coincidence and synchronicity. Webster's dictionary says that a coincidence is two events happening simultaneously as if by chance, but I don't see it as randomly as it is defined. The coincidence appears as if by chance, but as I see it, the work you've been doing on the truth and having the courage to pursue it invites and attracts opportunity. There is no coincidence, in other words but there is cause and effect. However, causes are not a linear, "do A to get to B" sequence. Goal-setting and action plans are linear and obvious causes of a result. Coincidence or synchronicity results from a different set of rules. The cause is not as obvious and logical. But as you will learn here, they can be just as reliable as the old methods of achievement.

Synchronicity alludes to the fact that things are aligning as they should. Webster's dictionary defines synchronicity as "events existing in a limited time period, ignoring historical antecedents." Again, not linear and logical.

You and your Life Blueprint are meant to be aligned, and when you do align with it, when you honor it, hear it, and/or catch up with it, you will experience things unfolding. Things just start to fall into place. As one of my workshop participants recently said: "You take one step; God will take two." If that is a better framework for you, use it.

Martina was amazed at the timing of an unlikely phone call she received. During her 90-day exploration, she made the difficult choice of uprooting her family to take a big job with her company. She had made up her mind that she could not say no, despite the hardship she felt she was going to cause her family. Just as she was about to accept her company's offer, her dream company called her out of the blue to explore getting her to come on board. Her dream company was right there in the city she was already in. She had not contacted them or even considered them as she pondered her choices. She could not believe her luck and the synchronicity of their call. Another miracle? Or maybe just things aligning as they are meant to.

Martina decided to commute to the job her original company offered, allowing her family to stay put. She wanted the time to feel the fit of her job while she kept the dialogue going with her dream company. At this writing, she was negotiating a deal to assume the ideal position back home.

If you feel at this point that things are not falling into place, you need to hear this: Sometimes they unfold in ways you might interpret as messy or less than perfect. Sometimes you'll see things happening that will cause you to question your luck. If luck is, in my definition, the reward for being responsible for the truth, what does it mean when things seem to be falling apart? It means that life is shaking out the cobwebs and doing some reshuffling before things can align properly.

Do you know people who have complained about their unhappiness in their job or marriage for years and then are utterly shocked when they are fired or their spouse up and leaves? Was it bad luck? And what was it that they were really shocked about? They wanted those things gone, they just did not have the courage to do something about the truth, so life took care of it for them. Rest assured, however, that in the end, they (and you) will probably find that even the mess was right on track.

For example, Gloria was a client in her late 50s. The perfect wife, mother, and social butterfly, she fit the mold of the dutiful spouse to a prominent man in the community. A couple years before beginning her work with me, she had gone back to school for her master's degree in health administration (she had been an RN). She was employed in an underpaid position at a university when we began working together. She came to find what was "next" for her career.

Gloria was not used to honoring the truth about what she wanted, but once she began to get in touch with it, she became stronger and stronger, was able to make some significant changes in her work situation, and even gained clarity about what direction would come next. That was the easy part, compared to what else ensued after she finally told the truth.

When we began working together, Gloria let me know that "Maybe, perhaps, my husband drinks a little too much in the evenings." I knew there had to be much more behind this teensy bit of truth. Without much prompting, Gloria agreed to begin attending Al-Anon meetings, where she began to learn about what she was really facing and how she had been contributing to it. Over the course of the next few weeks, things seemed to be getting worse as she revealed that her husband got home in the afternoons before her and would be in a robe with a few cocktails already imbibed when she arrived. The topper was when the family accountant called her into her office to let Gloria know that there was no money with which to pay the taxes and that if things did not get better soon, they were facing worse complications.

"Laura, my husband is an alcoholic," Gloria finally admitted.

"Yes, Gloria, he is. What are you willing to do?" I asked.

"I have to face him. I have to get him to tell the truth, too."

By now, you can interpret this story as Gloria's life falling apart if that is your point of view. Gloria did not see it that way, and neither did I. She felt bigger and stronger than ever. She had clarity unlike what she came into the 90-day process with. She marched into her husband's office and found out the truth about the money and how often he was showing up there or not. She put her house on the market so they could get some liquidity and find a more suitable, comfortable place that fit their empty-nester life better, and she got her husband into treatment. She became further determined to move her own career ahead and start making a decent salary, since her income was no longer just for play money. She finally admitted that she was a wasted talent, hiding out in the basement of the university's medical archives when she really belonged out in the world, helping to shape policy and improving the condition of health care in the world.

"Coincidentally," as she honored the real truth about herself, distinguished deans and policy-makers began inviting her to their homes and to appear at special events, and she began receiving recognition for her abilities and leadership.

Luck? Synchronicity? Gloria was becoming responsible for the truth! She removed the obstacles to the truth, allowed her "who" to come forth, and set her Life Blueprint in motion. It wasn't the smoothest ride. Synchronicity and hitting your sweet spot may not be a fairy tale, complete with magic dust and tinkly music, but they can be a journey to the core of your being that eventually results in a richness you were looking for all along.

Causality

At this point, you can start to expect the unexpected. Synchronicity and "coincidences" will occur. In fact, you can influence their occurrence. That is the easiest way to put yourself in opportunity's way. Expect it. Expect opportunity and cause it. Go into every new encounter or exploration of your area of interest with a child's wonder of what is possible. Writing your fiction in the last chapter was the beginning of transmitting that expectation to your immediate world. As we explored in Chapter Three when we dissolved your negative assumptions, you can expect the improbable because it is still possible somewhere out there in the ether. Even if you are wrong, even if your vision does not become a reality, having been open to it and expecting it will likely lead you to something else—perhaps something even better.

Oh, sure, this all sounds so very "icky, airy, fairy" and New-Age-y. But, somewhere deep down, you know it's true. If you only believed straight down to your toes that something was possible and then walked into the situation as if it were already so, then you would create an environment that can support positive results, even if they are not those you had on your radar screen.

Part of the reason the people I work with in 90-day stints accomplish so much in such a short time is because they expect to. The precedence has been set that the process works for a lot of my clients, so they trust that it can happen for them, they are willing to have that time frame work, and they come ready to take action.

A few have been disappointed, but only because the real work at hand (like addressing an issue in therapy or getting their financial life in order) showed up to knock their wish for clarity about the future out of first place. However, when they come to admit it, they know that is the gateway to the future they came to discover anyway.

The point is that when we expect something to happen and we construct a space emotionally, physically, mentally, and spiritually for it, we aid its manifestation. We can help cause it. Yes, unforeseen interruptions can happen, but for the most part, as we discussed earlier, expecting things to work out well will help them come to be. Doing your fiction writing and then engaging intuition as a guide to new clues helps prepare the space. Now comes the mental construct of expectation: expecting the new direction to take root in your life and to have a positive outcome and results. It's as if you mentally form a virtual-reality picture of the situation you want to create and then step into it. For the same reason that patients in clinical trials see improvements in their conditions even though they were given placebos, expectations play a role in outcomes.

Early in this book, I talked about the change that is occurring in us humans in what we want from our lives, and also the change in how we are defining ourselves as people. The five senses we have now only work in the physical world, and not in the world we are evolving to. Being able to embody more of who we are, and using our expanded brain capacity that is revealed to us more every day, will allow us to find satisfaction and fulfillment in today's world. There is a spiritual component here, and the use of a sixth sense will no longer be optional as we move forward. These are the tools that allow for the peace of mind and happiness you ultimately want to get from making a change.

We are longing for an easier way to live beyond the path that we have been taught is the road to hoe, and yet many of us have yet to explore what that new model may be. The concepts brought forth here are meant to show you that you have so much more to your makeup than you are using. Let this awareness be as much a part of your transition to a new life and a new direction as the actual physical changes that will occur in your environment as you make the change. Now, if you only take the time to be still long enough to visualize what you expect, you will find peace of mind and achieve a goal. Cool, huh?

> ### ▶ Exercise: *Set the Stage*
>
> Read this exercise through, and then do what it asks of you. Close your eyes and set the stage for your transition. See yourself already succeeding at your new direction. See yourself fully entrenched in it. Visualize it as a fait accomplis—it's already done, you're already there. Notice where you are, what you are doing, who you are with, what you are wearing, and, most important, what you are feeling.
>
> Pay attention to what it feels like, and remember that feeling. It will be what you will come to expect. That feeling is what you will look for and measure your success against as you move forward. The details of what you see may change, but the feeling must remain constant. The feeling is one where fear and joy become indistinguishable from each other.
>
> Remember that feeling! It's your new touchstone for knowing what's right for you.

Act As If

There is a fine line between delusions of grandeur and having the expectation that you will experience the best results. We are so afraid to put ourselves out there because we risk being wrong. To declare that you will be the first woman president and then have to live with not making it past the state senate, or to say you'll be CEO one day only to be stalled as the president of a division — God forbid we should be disappointed. Isn't that part of why we don't say it? Or is it that we are afraid of what people will think of us or say about us? Who cares? Setting your expectations high and behaving as if they're a given can only be a great asset to your cause. At the very least, you'll tickle the airwaves and educate the universe about how you expect it to respond to you. It's important to always set the stage so you can walk onto it, ready to play the part.

What do you need to do? If you were acting as though your transition had already occurred, what would you be doing differently?

Richard wanted his "next" to be moving into management at his company. He came to that conclusion after having been confused for a while about what he wanted. As soon as he discovered his "it," he took the challenge and started acting as though his transition had already occurred. Obviously, he did not have the authority to create change in his organization, but acting as though he did changed his behavior. Within two weeks of seeing it differently in his mind and being different in his body, he was recommended for an interview for a management position that was opening up. Synchronicity was at work once again. Although he did not end up getting the job, he still interpreted it as an immediate confirmation that he was on the right track. He did not have to struggle to keep up his new demeanor, so he continued to interview. As luck would have it, the first person to be offered the job turned it down, and Richard got it. After *wishing* for five years, acting "as if," got him what he wanted.

Madelyn shows us a different way of acting "as if." After working in corporate marketing for 25 years, Madelyn envisioned her "next" as being self-employed as a marketing consultant. As part of her plan to "act as if," she upgraded her hairstyle and wardrobe to really fit the part. Making these little changes gave her new confidence and made it much easier to begin to market herself as she grew her business.

Nicoletta wanted to write a book and needed to prepare for her new role as well. When she envisioned herself as a successful writer in the future, she saw that in the present, she needed a new computer and better office lighting to get started. She had a slow, outdated computer that was always crashing. She deserved better, and improving her office would be good preparation for her upcoming project.

> ### ▶ Exercise: *Act As If*
>
> Take pen to paper and take a moment to write down how you could "act as if" you were already 100 percent on the other side of your transition. Is there anything you need to do, be, have, or take on as part of the preparation for your transition? List those things, and then do them!

All these "act as if" preparations may sound easy enough to do, and they are, but do not underestimate their significance. They are part of getting providence rolling. When you demonstrate that you are ready, you will see more of your desired result. For example, you've heard it said that the rich only get richer. Have you ever noticed that people trip over themselves to give gifts of merchandise and travel to the rich? Logic would tell you that rich people can buy these things themselves. Why not give them to those who really need them? Besides the fact that they might experience the product and buy more, making the giveaway worth it, rich people have demonstrated their readiness to have. And have they will.

But which came first? The chicken or the egg? The readiness or the riches? It doesn't really matter. For us normal folks, taking the small but significant steps to "act as if" is in fact a demonstration of readiness to receive more. It is in taking action that we can influence the results. Unlike suffering over something we don't have yet or feel far from doing, there are things we can do now that can set the ball in motion.

Nicoletta did not wait until she had a book deal before she bought the computer. The book deal will come out of her demonstrating her readiness to have it. When Richard acted like a manager before he was one, it got him noticed as management material. Madelyn's looking and feeling good before she was ever successful in her own business made her a more attractive person to do business *with*.

Action, Action, We Want Action!

It's true that to a surprising degree you don't have to decide — life does it for you. However, you've also got to cooperate with life and take action! Your fiction gave you some hints as to what action you could take, and now we are going to make it concrete. But we are also going to make it *big*. Here's how I see it. You might as well stretch at this point in the game. It will help you to be braver and get perspective on much smaller things that scare you even more. When we go for the outrageous (the way we did when we wrote our fiction), it feels as though it's happening to somebody else, which allows for a healthy detachment and gives us the freedom to move forward.

One of my clients comes to mind. This client wanted to create a think-tank atmosphere and meeting space for people who like to discuss big ideas. He felt he was not yet at the point where the people he dreamed of having in the group would be equally interested in being with him. Logic would say that yes, he was probably right. However, his intuition and creativity had given him the idea. Being the most genuine source of inspiration there is, his idea had to have merit, so I challenged him to make a few phone calls to some of his dream think-tank participants. The first call he made was to a prominent couple, a renowned author and a master musician. Well, funny enough, they had been longing for a similar thing, and they agreed to set a date, offered their living room, and also began making phone calls.

So, there! Going for it is a far better way to get there than hoping that one day, some way, *somehow* it will happen.

We attract luck by telling the truth and taking action on it. Luck will most likely meet you halfway. Taking a *big* action and taking a risk will tempt fate even more.

▶ **Exercise:** *Make It BIG*

You have a time frame and a money investment (as discussed in Chapter Eight), and you have your fictitious scenarios and your "act as if" preparation, and now you have permission to think *big*. Get your timeline and take it up a notch. What is the *big* stretch that you can add to the mix? What would be beyond your wildest dream about what is possible? Add that to the plan and start taking action immediately. An example might be:

New direction: to live in New York City, pursuing a degree in design by the fall of next year.

The timeline action steps identified: Get an application, sign up for GEDs, go to NYC to search for an apartment, and put sketches in presentation format.

The "Think Big" Goal: In the best of all possible worlds, I get into New York's Fashion Institute of Technology and get an internship at Donna Karan New York.

Action for the outrageous part of the goal: Call Donna Karan New York to get the process rolling, find out who I know who knows DK herself or someone in her organization, research DKNY, and learn as much as I can about them.

If you've done your work in this chapter, I have no doubt that you have put yourself in opportunity's way and have begun to see some changes. The hardest part is done. Next, we will explore ways to ensure your success.

> **Questions to Ponder**

What experience do I have that tells me I am intuitive?

What will it take for me to rely on and apply my intuitive hunches?

What is something I know I need to do but may have ignored until now?

What would I have to change now to act as if my transition has already occurred?

What could I improve on when it comes to my ability to trust myself?

What is the feeling I will remember as the indication that I am in the right place?

What is the *big* action I need to take?

You Don't Have to Do It Alone

There are always difficulties arising that
tempt you to believe your critics are right.
— RALPH WALDO EMERSON

To multiply the number of opportunities available to you and your chances of succeeding at making a change, it makes sense to get other people involved in your quest. At the same time, it's wise to choose those people carefully. A support system is crucial to keeping you going; however, even if your own fears haven't crept up to deter you, you may have to deal with the fear that others project on you. In this chapter, we will address how to manage other people and how to overcome our tendency to go solo when we are evaluating our next step in life.

The Support System

Who is on your team? Who have you recruited to egg you on and catch you if you fall? Most people naturally have people in their life with whom they share their goings-on, and yet there is so much more room to make a support system a bigger and better designed part of your life.

Support can come in many forms, and it can reach you across state lines and even oceans. It does not depend on proximity. The key is putting some thought into recruiting and instructing the team. Your team will become your reservoir of courage, should you encounter further moments of doubt. It is a pool you want to dip into, so we have to be sure the right folks are in it.

Before choosing or confirming who your support system is, let's look at what support means to you. Do you need cheerleaders? Do you need people who can listen without judging or advising? Do you need a kick in the butt or a hug and a kiss from those on your team? Defining support is as important as having it.

Miguel had never really thought about what kind of support he wanted. He had just naturally fallen into a pattern of relying on his friends and family to hear him out when he needed to complain or, as he put it, "feel sorry for [him]self." When asked what kind of support would really be useful for him, he realized that he would probably feel better faster if his support system did not let him complain so much. Instead, he wanted them to help him turn his problems around and stop indulging his pity. He approached each of his usual supporters and let them know that the next time he called them to complain, they had his permission to remind him that he could do something about it. He then asked that they spend the time brainstorming with him instead of just listening to him. Now when he got stuck, he got out of it faster and found that he could do this for his friends as well. Miguel felt he was no longer an occasional burden to his supporters, and his relationships improved because of that.

All this may make you wonder what kind of support you provide those around you. Do you support them in their pain or in their power? Funny enough, not everyone wants to be supported to be their best. Some people actually get their needs met by staying frustrated or in pain. They get attention and sometimes sympathy, and they don't have to take responsibility for their problems. They may just like it that way. With that said, it may be difficult to understand why anyone would choose to support their friends and loved ones to be anything less than they can be, but it happens all the time. We get used to how people are, we forge behavioral patterns, and we forget that we can influence them. We also might feel too threatened at times to fully support someone. If supporting them means that they may move ahead of us, leave us, or otherwise do something that affects our life negatively, we might willingly (or unwittingly) become less supportive.

Being supportive does not necessarily mean that you only agree with the person you are supporting. However, it does mean that you are constructive and are not tearing the person down or being mean-spirited in your concern for them. It's OK to disagree or play devil's advocate, but it is imperative to have respect for the person and the situation they face.

If you turn it back around to how *you* would like to be supported, recognize that you can instruct—and, yes, sometimes even train—those around you to give you the support you need.

> **Exercise:** *Who Is on the Team?*

This exercise involves two steps: First, take some time to explore and write down what support means to you. What brings out your best, and what do you require from your support team to keep you positive and moving forward?

(Continued)

Exercise (*Continued*)

Second, take a moment to write down all the people in your life who support you now. Also add the names of people you'd like to have as part of your support team. Next to each person's name, note whether they support you in a way that really works for you. Also, write down the requests you need to make of each of them to make their support fit your definition and needs.

Example:

Supporter	Current Support	Future Support
Chris	good listener, good ideas, positive	no change
Teresa	sometimes overly critical, usually helpful	ask her to temper her criticism
Ben	all support is to him, not a giver	try to negotiate a change or take a break from him during my transition
Dory	Not on the team yet	would like her to mentor me

It may sound selfish to imagine instructing people on how they can support you. But it doesn't need to be selfish or sound empirious in any way. It may be unusual, but it is an example of being mindful and purposeful in making your life what you want

it to be. I'm sure you've heard many a CEO or leader say that
they succeed by surrounding themselves with a team of intelligent people. You are, in essence, building a team. You are not giving people direct pieces of your goal to accomplish for you, but
you are forming a team that can buoy you and keep you going.
Just as you would not expect a significant other to meet your every
need, neither will your support system members be uniquely
equipped for every function. Some may be better cheerleaders or
strategists, and others may be more useful for brainstorming or
hand-holding.

The opportunities to ask for their support may come as part of
a formal request or in your casual, everyday interactions. It may
mean asking them to lunch to help you with something or asking
them to hold you accountable for what you are trying to change,
or it may just mean asking them to speak to you differently if they
have indeed said something insensitive.

At the risk of sounding insensitive myself, people, like puppies,
are trainable. You can set boundaries, correct behavior, and redirect their negativity—all for the good of your new life direction
and the future of your relationship with that person.

Setting Boundaries

Where is your line in the sand when it comes to people's behavior toward you? Do you let them do as they wish, even if it is
hurtful or disrespectful to you? Do you recognize where they end
and you begin, and have a clear line that they are not allowed to
cross? That is what a boundary is—an imaginary line that keeps
you safe from purposeful or inadvertent harm brought on by another's words or actions. Are you aware of yours?

Think of the people who are in your support system. Is there something they say or do that you find yourself needing to talk about or review with other friends? Is there something you keep letting slide that bothers you about how you interact with each other? Is there a part of your relationship with them that is difficult, that the two of you have never addressed? That place that bugs you may be a place where you need to draw a boundary.

Let's say someone in your life is critical of the change you are considering, or they feel the need to share every pitfall that might be awaiting you as you make your transition. Would you say that is supportive? Probably not, so the boundary will need to be set that the behavior is not OK with you.

This is where a lot of people get nervous. "Who am I to tell someone what they can and cannot say?" I've heard people ask. But you have a choice. You can let this person poison your thoughts, or you can take a break from seeing them or simply address the issue. You have the right to tell people what you can and cannot tolerate. It's how you say it that makes the difference.

Correcting Behavior

There is one sentence that has made all the difference to the people I work with when they need to set a boundary or redirect someone's behavior. It helps to delineate the past from the future, and the missteps from the right steps, without blame or guilt. This is the sentence: "In the past, you've been used to me _____, but that's not OK with me anymore, so from now on you can count on me to _____."

So you might say, "In the past, you've been used to me laughing and acting cavalier when you tear apart my ideas, but that's not OK with me anymore, so from now on you can count on me to stop the criticism before it begins," or, "In the past, I've let our habit of one-upping each other slide, but that's not OK with me anymore, so from now on you can count on me not to respond when we fall into that game."

It's important to point out what the infraction is and then make a clear and specific statement about what direction you would like to guide your interactions with this person. Obviously, you can use any words you like, but the above framework helps spell it out. And if your efforts don't lead to a resolution, you may have to find someone else for your support team.

Keeping Naysayers at Bay

Please understand that when people react strongly to you or your plans, ultimately those reactions are about them and their "stuff" vs. really being about you. The changes you're moving toward might remind them of changes they would like to make but are unable to set in motion. There is room for you to explore what responsibility you can take for the way they reacted, but also remember that you may be bringing up an issue for them, and you should not take their reaction to heart.

This leads me to the question of whether it is OK to share your desires with people, or if they are better kept a well-protected secret. There is a school of thought that says there is power in keeping your deepest desires and dreams close to your vest, allowing them to multiply in intensity within you. But I feel that when you share your innermost desires with the people who truly want the best for you, the result is more ease in getting to where you want to go. You want people in place who can be positive mirrors of your expectations. Those expectations you set in the last chapter can be shared with those who can truly support you.

On the other hand, you should keep your desires away from

those who might poison them, although they may not do so intentionally. There will be people with whom sharing your plans is not wise. You want to avoid the people who will echo your deepest fears.

A dear friend of mine was engaged to be married for the second time to the same man. She was just a mere three weeks away from her wedding day, when she had her umpteenth conversation with one of her friends as to whether she was doing the right thing by getting married. She loved her fiancé, but they were long past the heady stage of romance. They had had some confusing times, and she was questioning herself.

When my turn came to be called on for support, I heard all the things that this friend had said, and it was so clear why this person in particular was sending my friend further into doubt. She was echoing every fear and confirming every doubt that my friend had. I pointed that out and suggested that she only talk to the people who supported her decision to get married. But she did not do that and ended up canceling the wedding.

A couple years went by, but my friend did eventually marry this man (and happily so—they now have two lovely children). Unfortunately, it took the death of her father for her to find the strength of her own convictions and realize that this wonderful man was still in her life for a reason. We all looked forward to the wedding, but a lot of us had to admit that we did not cut the tags off our new clothes until the day of the ceremony, just in case.

This is a call for parents to heed as well. Watch where your fears for your children taint their ability to follow their Life Blueprint. We only want the best for them, and yet we can so often cripple them with our fears and even cause doubts where there were none before. It's understandable to be afraid if your child wants to get involved in a contact sport or if your daughter wants to pursue her dreams in a city far away from you, but how can you be constructive and supportive, even through the veil of your own fear?

Guide your children to find examples of people who did what they want to do, or have them speak to people who can educate them on what it takes to reach their dreams. They'll be smart enough to figure out whether they want it badly enough, and whether they can endure those things you fear they'll have to go through. When people I know have kids who want to break into theatre, they send them to me. I answer their questions and keep my opinion to a minimum, and they choose for themselves if it's right for them. But if you do not allow it to be their own discovery, you'll have clipped their wings and limited their growth. When advising anyone, keep your own fears in check and expect others to do the same for you.

"But what if they are right? How do I know?" Are you wondering how to know if other people's doubts and fears are more than just supportive signs that you are off track? Early on in this book, I said that even if everyone tells you that you are crazy, that's not overwhelming evidence that it is true. Even having everyone you know tell you that they can't support your decision may not be enough evidence to declare them right and you wrong. The bottom line is this: If you find yourself becoming defensive, angry, or highly emotional, it would be a good idea to double-check your true feelings with yourself. Your naysayers may have hit on something you need to re-examine. On the other hand, while you might feel hurt that you don't have the support of the folks who matter to you, if it does not interfere with your free fall, you are tapping your Life Blueprint and should feel confident proceeding.

If you're still wondering if the naysayers are right, you can try the following exercise.

> ## Exercise: *The "So What?" Game*

Try this with the next naysayer that you encounter (even if that naysayer is you!). Let the person know that you'd like them to engage in an exercise with you. Your tone of voice is important to the game. Keep it playful, light, and curious. An angry, defensive, or sarcastic tone will defeat the game's effectiveness.

After each objection or fear that your naysayer presents, ask: "So what?" You can also substitute "so what" for "then what will happen?" Here's an example.

Someone says: "You are going to lose so much money!"

You ask: "So what?"

They ask: "Don't you care if you lose money?"

You ask: "So what if I lose money?"

They ask: "You'll deplete your investments—it'll be terrible."

You ask: "So what?"

They ask: "You'll be in a bad position!"

You ask: "So what?"

Keep asking "so what?" until your naysayer can no longer hold the logic of his opposing viewpoint. The game can sometimes get ridiculous as the naysayer struggles to keep his argument. He might blurt out in frustration: "You'll die!" Bring it to a close, thank the person for caring about you, and then check in with yourself to see if the game helped you shed some of your concerns. If the naysayer (or you) does hit on a consequence that stumps you, it will become a good place to explore and re-evaluate. At the very least, this game should serve to bring some humor and break through some of your fears.

Beth played the "so what?" game with her naysaying husband and neglected to mention that it was a game. Her tone escalated as her husband's frustration with her grew. He thought she didn't care about him or their life and was mocking him. It blew up in her face. Marcella, on the other hand, kept lightness in the game and was able to move her naysaying sister from foe to friend. Her sister saw that Marcella's resolution to move to the beach and become a freelance journalist instead of being a magazine employee was not going to break her bank account, isolate her from her family, or keep her from meeting eligible men—all things her sister feared would happen if Marcella pursued her new direction. The game also revealed Marcella's sister's true resistance to the change. Her sister was afraid to lose her connection to Marcella if she moved away, and that was her true motivation for being a naysayer. But she was not conscious of it until the game brought out the truth.

Asking for Help

I have made a huge assumption in this chapter. I have assumed that you are the kind of person who would ask for help in the first place. By this point in the book, it is not the first time that I've asked you to include other people in your quest, but it is the first time that the request could have long lasting implications or benefit to certain relationships.

Most people assume they have to do things by themselves. Either they are type A and they don't believe anyone could really be helpful and offer solutions in a way that is palatable to them, or they are ashamed to ask for help. Still others are so used to doing things on their own that it would not even cross their mind to look for help. Do any of these describe you? If they do, try to think about who you would interpret yourself to be if you asked for help. If you think you'd appear weak or out of control or needy, I wonder if people appear that way to you when they ask you for help. If they don't, then why would you?

So many people suffer unnecessarily or are stuck interminably for the simple reason that they assume they must do things alone. They think, *Why would anyone want to help me with that?* One universal example that comes to mind is almost as life-altering as pursuing a new direction in your life. Wherever I have traveled in the world, a predominant majority of the audiences I speak to will admit, with some prodding, that they have unruly clutter in their homes. It is a cause of shame and serious deterrent to joy for a lot of people. It is something that they try to bury and ignore, but ultimately there is a cost to people's stress level, depth of joy, social interaction, and the feeling of peace that comes with being at home.

Their biggest obstacle to removing clutter is that they do not ask for help. Whether it be the shame involved or just that people cannot fathom anyone else wanting to help with something that is so dreadful to them, people assume it is up to them and only them to eliminate clutter. Maybe some will hire a personal organizer, but most put up with the problem. I kid with my audiences and say that we could take the hundreds of them, house to house, to every audience member's home and get all the clutter-busting done in 48 hours. They laugh, but they get that they could conquer their mess if they let others help.

If asked correctly, most people love to help. They like to be the hero of sorts, or they enjoy being helpful and of service and useful. Who wouldn't? So let people help.

There are ways to make it go more smoothly. Just think of your own preferences. Wouldn't you find it easier to help someone who is taking initiative and has done their homework vs. someone who is behaving in a somewhat helpless way and is depending on you? I would venture to say you would. So, consider *who* you have to be to get the best assistance you can. If it is not utter desperation that you are in, and you can take charge of how you ask for help, then by all means do. It will go a long way toward getting what you need.

A client of mine was finding herself procrastinating about getting her financial paperwork in order during this process, and she bucked when I asked her to get someone to help her. She wondered why anyone would agree to do so. She assumed she would just get no for an answer, so she did not even try. I asked her if she'd do it for a friend, and she said yes. So she quickly turned herself around, and thought about at what stage she would have liked to join someone else's project. She decided that she could gather all the papers and have them spread out on the living room floor, and that she'd like her friend to come and help arrange them in categories, do the math with her, and put them away in neat and organized files. Her dread turned to fun as she put herself out to ask for help.

Making It Fun

Building a support system does not need to be serious and poker faced business. It can be a blast if you get creative about it. I've even had clients launch their new directions with theme parties—the singer giving a living room concert, the investment whiz passing out lottery tickets to snag his first clients, the would-be novelist having his friend submit funny family stories to inspire him while beginning his novel, and the new business owner launching his business with a casino night as he rolled the dice and tried his luck at a new venture. The lighter the atmosphere, the more fun your supporters will have and the more memorable the beginning of your adventure will be. You are also creating a tangible way for people to be a part of your venture before you have to ask for too many heavy favors. People will be invested and will want you to succeed, especially if they feel as though they are part of your venture.

Getting like-minded folks together with a unifying goal (like your goal in exploring a new direction for your life) can also prove to be a fun way to have support in your life. There are Life Blueprint groups (see Appendix One) and other kinds of groups that people form to put good supporters around them. It is not hard to do, and it's wonderfully selfish. Put together a group of people that have similar concerns, and you have built-in support while also giving it to others. The clutter-busting brigade is sounding like a good idea, isn't it?

It only takes three people to be a group, so don't worry about recruiting a big team. Another idea is to buddy up with someone else who is also making major life changes. Check in with each other every day or every other day to keep the momentum going for both of you.

Getting other people involved and making it fun will benefit you more than you know. Having fun, laughing, and having support to fall back on will keep your transmitters in good shape and will help luck continue to be yours. This does not have to be hard.

> **Questions to Ponder**

What did I learn about what support means to me?

What can I now see about the people who support me in my life?

Who do I need to add to my support team?

What boundaries do I need to set and with whom?

Which behaviors of those in my support team needs correcting? What can I do that I could not do before to correct it?

Who do I have to be to ask for help?

What will I do to make this fun?

Chapter Twelve

Following Your Life Blueprint

Courage is the price life exacts for granting peace.

—AMELIA EARHART

Believe it or not, we have come to the end of the road. This is where you pick up and I let off. Most of you will be so far into your discoveries that there is no turning back, and no matter how long it takes or how long you put it off, you will have to do something about them. The truth is undeniable. This is where you will follow the blueprint that has been set out for you.

Others will be at the point of discovering "it," and the same goes for them. If it took you until now to find "it," then go back and use Part Two as it was intended. It will spell out what to do with your discoveries, and when you get here the second time, you too will be ready to follow the blueprint.

Now What? promises a new direction or vision for yourself, and some of you may even be fully engaged in transitioning to your new direction by this time. No matter which category you fall into, congratulations. You have done the hard work: the exploration, the digging, the imagining, the expecting, and taking action, and they are all accomplishments. Anything that brings you closer to knowing yourself will serve you well as you move forward.

Where Are You Now?

You've come a long way. You've let go of the parts of the past that keep you blocked and have taken stock of the good parts of the past that will form your future. You have taken a good, hard look at the beliefs that gave birth to many self-imposed limits, and you have the tools to use to bust through them. You have uncovered a sense of purpose and have recognized the unique contribution that you make, understanding that it is the turnkey to all you want to accomplish. You've identified possible new paths, if not decided on one. You have researched and have familiarity with what it will take to adopt your new life. You've reconciled with your money and have come to some decisions about how your money can help you move forward. You've created a timeline. You have stretched yourself to think big and are taking action accordingly. You may have found a way to include intuition in your quest. You understand the importance of defining support, asking for it, and getting it. Your job now is to champion progress and keep things moving forward.

Before we go, here is one last exercise to help you chart the course to your new destination or vision.

> ### Exercise: *Setting the Course*

You created your fictitious timeline earlier, and you took some pieces of it as insight and action that you can put to use. Here I would like you to create a plan for the next six months to a year.

Take pen to paper once more and write down the name of each month in its own column across the top of a page. Take it one year out or six months out from where you are now, depending on how close you are to achieving progress in your new direction (six months if you are close, one year if you are still in progress). First, mark the six-month and one-year months with a celebratory milestone you want to see by that date. Then go back and fill in the months with action steps and benchmarks that must be met to bring you to those celebration moments.

Read this calendar often, and be sure you are implementing the steps. Even if you falter, read it *daily*. Writing things down and seeing them often does wonders for your ability to achieve them. Sometimes it results in things happening with seemingly no effort at all. (Remember, I said *sometimes*, no promises!)

One Thing a Day

When I was an actress/waitress, I had a daily mantra. It was: Do one thing a day toward the dream. No matter how down I was, or how busy I was, or how futile it sometimes felt, I always did one thing a day toward the dream. It might have been an audition, a phone call to a potential agent, letters to casting directors, postcards to people I'd worked for before, learning a new song, taking a lesson, and the list went on. However, I was stubborn and not heeding the call that I was off my Life Blueprint, but the rule still worked for the better. It has become a rule that I have repeated to clients over the years.

When people say, "But, I'm so busy," or, "I hope I don't lose my momentum after the 90 days," I always remind them to do one thing a day. And that is what I want you to hear, especially if you are still juggling a lot of balls in your life and now, undeniably, have to add this transition you are making. You may even be dragging your research project along from Chapter Seven, and now I'm challenging you with more. Not to worry, just keep the daily focus. One step at a time is enough to put you in opportunity's way.

Who vs. What

If you leave this process with only one thing, I want you to leave it understanding that *who* you are is more important than *what* you do. Getting to be truly yourself will make you happier than any dream job, dream mate, or dream house that requires you being someone other than your true self. It is also your ticket out of a less-than-satisfying job or life situation, and it is the key to your future path. Develop yourself, take time for yourself, trust your instincts and wishes, and realize that no one can take anything from you that was ultimately meant for you. Your satisfaction will not stem from *what* you do, but from *who* you get to be while you do that thing.

Karen, our executive who thought she had to be VP before she could have her own business, came to the end of the 90 days knowing clearly that being all of who she was meant moving ahead with her dream. When we parted ways, she was entertaining two different offers to become the CEO of a small business.

This, she felt, would let her express all of who she was and would allow her to learn even more without risking her own business. She was ready to take the leap.

Janelle, our CPA, had a new sense of herself that made her so happy that she wasn't immediately concerned with knowing what was next. She wanted to enjoy her newfound self and her new-found happiness, and let the answers stem from there.

Within a month of finishing his 90 days, Steve was so jazzed by being clear about who he was and what he needed to get out of working that he found himself with opportunities that he did not even feel he had outwardly pursued. One of his favorite vendors was eager to discuss Steve joining the company. At the same time, some other colleagues began talking about starting an investment firm together. A few months later, Steve let me know that his current company was considering starting an in-house investment firm and had identified him as a potential leader. The last time we talked, which was six months after he had completed the 90 days, he was negotiating a big promotion.

I had mentioned Steve earlier as someone who had been miserable for more than six years and who could not figure out what he wanted to do. It wasn't until he figured out *who* he was and *who* he needed to be that he got some answers about what he wanted to do. When he was clear, opportunities came to him.

Set Yourself Up to Win

This time of progress is an important time to make sure you are taking care of yourself. Persistence requires patience, and patience requires that you avoid being hard on yourself. Take time to relax or do something fun during the weeks of progress. Be careful to keep your self-esteem and success coffers full by tapping into your support system and giving yourself plenty of credit for the actions you are taking, regardless of the outcome.

Marabel Morgan, author of *The Electric Woman*, once said, "Persistence is the twin sister of excellence. One is a matter of quality; the other, a matter of time." You have journeyed in a new direction for your life, and you will not falter. It may take time, but probably less time than you think. There is a whole slew of people on a similar quest, and they want you to succeed at making this transition. If you do, it means they can. So forge the path to a new life direction and know that the peace you experience is a contribution to making this world a better place for us all. What has brought you here is the power of your Life Blueprint guiding you to heed your soul's call. This is part of your personal evolution; there is no wrong choice. Every turn in the road will add up to something useful. There is no question that life sometimes offers bumps and bruises, but they come so we can appreciate the beauty of what we already have. By entering this 90-day process, you have engaged in being fully alive. Fear is appropriate, and excitement is even more so. I hope that I've helped deliver you to yourself. Now, you take it from here. Good luck.

Final Thoughts

I wrote the first draft of this book in 90 days. That is an unprecedented record for me. I wrote my last two books over the course of nine months, delivering my manuscripts with my first child and a set of twins, respectively. There is something to be said for writing a book without being pregnant. It's *grrrrreat!*

Thanks to the beta-testing groups that were awaiting each chapter as it came out of my computer, I stayed on course and learned so much from them as I went along. This book held some personal growth for me as well. I discovered, shared, and broke through my own money bugaboo, and in teaching others how to find the significant themes in their personal histories, I found myself sharpening my own ability to do so even further. But probably most significant was telling the truth about the new life directions that call to me.

For a few years now I have had this notion in the back of my mind that I would spend my retirement (a long time from now) working as a minister. Since this inkling has become more persistent over time, it has become more and more of a front-burner vs. a back-burner exploration. I looked at it as an analogy instead of a true path for my life. After all, I often feel like my work can be compared to a ministry because of the fervent passion I can feel for it. The sense of seeing it as an analogy only lasted a few months. So I went through what I call a "quickie ordination," and I can now legally perform weddings in the United States. But that wasn't enough to satisfy the emerging message from my Life Blueprint. I can already feel the pull to get an advanced degree or further training.

The other notion that I had to be truthful about during the work on this book was about pushing the envelope on intuition and having to admit that there is a higher form of it. I am psychic. People usually think I am joking when I say it, but I am not joking. I say it to test the waters, really.

About eighteen months ago, I had a heated discussion with my friend, Dr. Sonia Choquette. Sonia has been a practicing psychic for more than thirty years and is the author of several wonderful books that help people get in touch with their psychic abilities, including *The Psychic Pathway*. Our argument stemmed from our different definitions of what it means to be psychic. She defines psychic as "of the soul," and although I did feel that my work was highly, highly intuitive, I did not feel comfortable saying I was psychic. I did not experience myself that way. She insisted that I was psychic and that I do use it in my work.

That conversation with Sonia never left me. As I watched myself with clients that I had begun to work with in only 90-day stints, I had to wonder what else was at work besides more than a decade of experience that allowed people such huge leaps in such a short time. Coaching is not designed to tell people what to do or to prescribe a formula for their life, but I did find that I tuned in to people differently and would ask different questions than I had before. If psychic indeed means "of the soul," then my work was about something deeper, as I always felt it was. Eventually, I did come back to Sonia and ask her to mentor me so I can be even more useful to the people I work with.

I share this with you to hopefully provide an example of how we continue to grow even if we are happy and successful right where we are—to show you how our "it" will continue to evolve as we do.

Am I shutting down my coaching company and putting out my minister/psychic shingle? No. I am using both disciplines, which my Life Blueprint has brought me, to enhance the package I am in now. The time may come for a more defined switch, but I know now is not the time. Nonetheless, although life often brings you opportunities and makes your decisions for you, "coincidence" would have it that I have been invited to substitute for a renowned minister and deliver my first sermon before the end of this year. Life is always an adventure, isn't it?

I do see perfection in what calls to me now. More and more, I feel that my work *ministers* to the soul. If I am to continue to be a teacher and require being a step ahead of the people I am meant to work with, then it makes sense to me that these areas of concentration have shown up for me. I have said throughout this book that the evolution of the people who read it prepares them to be more sixth-sensory in dealing with the demands of their life. So I have to be ready for them by honoring what is true for me. It cannot be a secret that I operate on a sixth-sensory platform if I expect others to embrace it in their lives as well.

Thank you for coming on the 90-day journey with me. It is always an honor and a privilege to be included in your growth.

Resources and Nuts and Bolts to Facilitate Change

> *Let us never negotiate out of fear. But let us never fear to negotiate.*
> —JOHN F. KENNEDY

Many of the ideas discussed in the book may require further investigation or details. Here are some leads and tips that could help you make your new direction a reality.

Negotiating a Leave of Absence

Previously called a "sabbatical," a personal leave of absence (LOA), is an option for getting some time off without losing the opportunity to return to your current position or company. You should review your company's employee handbook or contact your human resources department to get the details about any LOA policies.

Make sure this is a viable option for you before you speak with your manager. Find out the parameters of the policy, such as allowed length of leave, who needs to approve it, its impact on your benefits or seniority, and the reasons a leave may be granted. Companies will often consider requests for LOAs for reasons such as employee or family member illness or injury; maternity, paternity, or adoption leave; military service; pursuing a degree or specialized training; professional internships or work-study programs; or volunteer or community-service activities.

Your success in obtaining a leave of absence is dependent on creating a compelling business case. The success of your plan and getting an LOA approved is to establish how it will benefit both you and the company. For example, if you plan to study something that will improve your performance or give you new skills that benefit the company, you should include that as part of your case. You want to be sure to include how your work will be handled in your absence. Be creative. Discuss several alternatives that show that your absence will create the least amount of disruption for the company, your manager, your coworkers, your customers, etc.

Even if you anticipate needing to be gone longer than your company's policy allows, it's best to apply anyway. Circumstances can change—you may decide to return early, or perhaps you can negotiate an extension. With most personal LOAs, you will not receive any paid company benefits. However, you can often continue in your current medical and dental plans at your own expense, and you usually retain credit for your years of service. This is a big advantage, especially if you are seriously considering returning to the company. The company will generally hold your position open, or commit to providing a similar job (at similar pay and benefits) when you return. If you are approved for a leave of absence, it is important that you understand who you must stay in touch with and how often. This ongoing communication throughout your LOA is critical.

Paid Time Off

Another variation is to request to take advantage of stockpiled vacation days, sick time, holidays, or other paid time off under your company's policies. This is usually an option if you need a shorter period away from work. Your human resources department can advise you about options in this area.

Books

Six Months Off: How to Plan, Negotiate, and Take the Break You Need Without Burning Bridges or Going Broke by Hope Dlugozima and others. (This book is out of print, but Amazon.com carries used copies, and you may find it in your local library.)

Time Off from Work: Using Sabbaticals to Enhance Your Life While Keeping Your Career on Track by Lisa Rogak (Wiley, 1994).

Negotiating Severance or an Early Retirement Package

If your plan necessitates that you leave your position or your company entirely, you should examine whether it is an option for you to receive severance pay or an early retirement package. These programs are generally offered during times when a company is going through significant change, such as a merger, acquisition, or reorganization, or during challenging economic periods, such as a downturn in economy or business performance. It is important to research whether your company has a formal severance or retirement program, your eligibility for it, and the details of the program. If your company does not have a formal program, you should still try to negotiate this. The place to start is with your immediate boss, or your boss's boss. Your human resources department should also be able to consult with you about your options in this area. Severance/retirement programs often contain one or more of the following components:

➤ A onetime monetary payment (or period of continued salary), usually based on factors such as your position in the company and years of service. This amount may or may not be negotiable.

➤ Continued medical and dental benefits: if they're not offered, you can try to negotiate the same or similar company contributions as those you received as an employee.

➤ Outplacement assistance, including services such as resume preparation, interviewing training and support, or support in pursuing continuing education.

➤ Letters of reference or recommendation, detailing your positive job performance.

In most states in the United States, you may receive unemployment pay benefits in addition to any severance pay, either at the same time or upon completion of your company's severance program.

Timing is an important factor in pursuing a severance or retirement package. You must pursue this option *prior* to announcing your plans to resign. Volunteering to be laid off or being proactive in seeking a package may have serious implications to your career if you don't ultimately end up leaving the company. However, if you have either direct information or an intuition that your job may be impacted, you should consider this a very viable option.

If your company is actively laying off employees and they know you want to volunteer to leave, it is likely that the company will work with you to make this happen. This benefits the company by allowing them to retain another employee who wants to stay but would have otherwise have been let go. Generally speaking, the longer your tenure with a company, the better your negotiating power in this area.

Where possible, you should try to control the timing of your exit from your company. Try to negotiate a date at least four to twelve weeks out. This allows you ample time to properly complete or transition your work, as well as to communicate to your colleagues your reasons for leaving. These are both important things to care for as you leave your company.

Be cautious about signing a noncompete agreement, or a release-of-legal-claims document. Unfortunately, some companies will not provide severance benefits without your signature on such documents, but you should read them carefully, because they may potentially limit your options for the future.

Although it seems counter-intuitive, your company may be open to rehiring you in a consulting capacity, even after you have retired or received a severance package. If you think you might be interested, you should discuss this prior to leaving your position.

Books

Fired, Downsized, or Laid-Off: What Your Employer Doesn't Want You to Know by Alan Sklover, a compensation attorney.

Job Rights and Survival Strategies: A Handbook for Terminated Employees by Paul H. Tobias and Susan Sauter, which is available from the nonprofit National Employee Rights Institute (NERI) in Cincinnati, by calling (800) 469-7374. Mr. Tobias is chairman of and Ms. Sauter is an attorney with NERI.

Negotiating a Telecommuting Arrangement

Once a practice of only the most progressive employers, telecommuting is now one of the most popular ways to provide flexibility in the workplace. More than thirty million people in the United States work from home some or all of the time. This option offers many advantages to an employer, including reduced costs (such as reduced need for office space), and is highly beneficial to the employee as well (no commute, informal work environment, etc.). However, some jobs lend themselves better to this option. For example, a supervisor needs to be present in the work location of his or her employees, while a computer programmer can work very effectively from a remote location.

Successful telecommuting requires superior focus and time-management skills. Many people have tried and failed at this, finding that they are too distracted by the home environment. In addition, one of the biggest complaints of those who have gone this path is a feeling of isolation. A downside to telecommuting is that you have very limited personal contact and social interaction, and are often far removed from the day-to-day happenings of the company and shut off from the company "grapevine." However, the upside far outweighs the challenges with this career option, and it just may be the perfect solution for you.

Websites

➤ Learn more about the real scoop on working from home at www.workathomesuccess.com, where you can also find how to write a work-at-home proposal for your company.

➤ www.workathomesuccess.com/telecomm.htm links to job search sites for people who want to work from home.

➤ www.workingfromanywhere.org.ITAC (International Telwork Association & Council) is a nonprofit organization dedicated to advancing the growth and success of work, independent of location. ITAC sponsors Telework America and other research, holds educational events, distributes publications, disseminates information about telework, and assists businesses and the public in optimizing the advantages of working remotely.

Books

Jobs at Home: A Complete Guide to Finding or Creating a Work-at-Home Job by Leslie Truex.

Teleworking and Telecommunting by Jeffery D. Zbar (Made Ez Products, 2002).

101 Tips for Telecommuters: Successfully Manage Your Work, Team, Technology and Family by Debra A. Dinnocenzo (Berret-Koehler, 1999).

Mompreneurs Online: Using the Internet to Build Work at Home Success (Perigee, 2001).

Negotiating a Flexible Schedule or Job Share

Another way to get creative in making changes to your work life is to consider a flexible schedule or job-sharing arrangement. If you think your employer would never go for this option, consider this:

➤ 88 percent of Fortune 1000 companies offer part-time schedules, 77 percent offer flextime, and 48 percent offer job sharing.

➤ 20 percent of the 20 million part-time workers in America are in professional positions.

➤ 95 percent of all employees who participate in job-sharing are women.

➤ 26 percent of all employed women work part-time.

These figures are from www.athomemothers.com, the website of the National Association of At Home Mothers. This website also features numerous links to other websites that offer information on how to negotiate various benefits (flextime, job sharing, etc.). It pertains to men too.

Like other options, flexible schedules offer many benefits to both a company and an employee. By offering flexible or nontraditional schedules, companies can get employees to work during times when their business would otherwise come to a halt. In addition, flexible schedules are a way for companies to gain additional resources during peak business hours, reducing costs such as overtime pay. For you, flextime offers the freedom of a work schedule that's structured around your life, instead of a life scheduled around your work.

However, this type of arrangement requires you to do your homework. You should expect to need to sell your idea to your current employer, since most are hesitant to enter into this kind of work arrangement. To do this, you need to develop a viable plan that demonstrates that your employer's needs will be met, along with your own. You should develop a proposal that demonstrates how the flexibility you are suggesting—evening hours, compressed work schedule, working at home—will benefit you and your company.

Here are some suggestions for developing a successful proposal:

➤ Understand your company's current policies regarding alternative work arrangements.

➤ Seek support from your supervisor or coworkers—if the approval of your plan is dependent on your immediate supervisor, or someone that is one or more levels above him/her, this is *critical*. In addition, it helps you identify any issues or objections up front, so you can address them in your proposal.

➤ Find others inside or outside of your company who have successfully negotiated a flexible schedule, and learn what worked (and what didn't work) for them.

➤ Identify ways that your company will benefit from your proposal—such as minimizing turnover, increasing productivity, or otherwise saving money as a result of approving your suggestion.

➤ Identify and address any and all concerns you anticipate—don't avoid the questions or objections that you know will be raised—better to deal with these up front than have to react to them later.

➤ Create a proposal that articulates the specifics of your plan
and how you will be successful. This might include a sum-
mary of your recommendation (including your reason for
making the proposal), your performance history, your research
data (internal and external), supervisor/coworker input, and
your recommendation (hours worked, job responsibilities,
flexibility, compensation, etc.).

Job sharing is another alternative to a traditional work schedule, especially if you are looking for a professional or management level position on a part-time basis. This option is easiest to
sell to your employer when you have already identified a job-
share partner with whom to share your responsibilities. Next, you
need to make the case that two can do the job as well as one. To
make job sharing successful, it's important that both employees
have similar skills and work habits, and that you have a relationship of open, honest communication. Job sharing requires both
employees to be somewhat flexible and to occasionally work additional hours; when there are two of you, employers often expect
coverage for vacations, leaves of absences, etc.

Website
➤ www.opm.gov/LMR/html/flexible.asp. The website of the
United States Office of Personnel Management will give you
all the legal know-how you would ever want about flexible
and compressed work schedules.

Executive Temping

In recent years, more and more companies are utilizing temporary employees at the executive level to fill their leadership

voids. Experienced, senior-level leaders can find work on anything from a short-term project or initiative to a year-long contract, filling in while a company searches for a full-time executive. Companies will generally look for an individual who is highly experienced and has previously held one or more executive positions in other companies. The key is to hit the ground running and be able to add value right away.

Book
Executive Temping : A Guide for Professionals by Saralee Terry Woods.

Websites
➤ The Directory of Temporary Placement Firms for Executives, Managers & Professionals, found at www.kennedyinfo.com/js/xtemp.html.
➤ Check out www.monster.com for temporary placement opportunities besides executive positions.

Positioning Yourself for a New Field

If you are considering a complete career change into a position where you have limited direct experience, it is important to know that you have more options than most people think. Most people assume that they will have to take a cut in pay and, while this might be true, to enter a new field, it is not necessary to affect your overall compensation. There are other things you can ask for, and there are other things you can do to demonstrate your commitment to make it worth a company's while to give you a generous compensation plan. Some tips include:

➤ Be able to clearly articulate your transferable skills (that is, if you worked in finance and want to get into marketing, you have analytical skills that will help you work through budgets).

➤ Articulate your commitment to bridging the gap in your experience (going to school, taking training, extra hours).

➤ Don't rest on past experience; paint a picture of what you think you can deliver.

At the point of receiving an offer, keep in mind that you do not have to sacrifice your overall compensation.

➤ Instead of a straight pay cut, negotiate a win-win bonus (based on performance).

➤ You do not have to start from scratch on vacation time. Ask to maintain the weeks you have now.

➤ Other areas of compensation should be kept in mind: health care, dental, childcare, sick days, etc.

➤ Build in other incentives for yourself and the company that will yield further compensation.

Books

101 Salary Secrets: How to Negotiate Like a Pro (Ten Speed Press, 2001) by Bernard Haldane.

Get More Money on Your Next Job: 25 Proven Strategies for Getting More Money, Better Benefits and Greater Job Security (McGraw-Hill, 1997) by Lee E. Miller.

Dynamite Salary Negotiation: Know What You're Worth and Get It (Impact Publications, 1993) by Ronald Krannich, Ph.D.

Starting a Small Business

If you have an area of expertise that makes you marketable, being a business owner may be an excellent option for you. More and more people are choosing this option in order to have more control over their work, their finances, and their time. However, a new business is a huge undertaking, and to be successful, you must do your homework. Running a business can mean working 24/7, especially in the start-up stage. The financial challenges of establishing a business, coupled with the lack of benefits and compensation, make it critical that you have a solid plan. Owning and operating your own business requires great risk, but it offers great benefits in return.

Website

➤ Lots of information is available on the Small Business Association website: www.sba.gov/starting. It outlines first steps, how to write a business plan, and financing information. You can also print out a small business resource guide (about 39 pages).

Books

How to Start and Run Your Own Corporation: S-Corporations for Small Business Owners by Robert A. Cooke.

Home-Based Business for Dummies by Paul Edwards.

Working from Home: Everything You Need to Know About Living and Working Under the Same Roof by Paul and Sarah Edwards.

Why Aren't You Your Own Boss: Leaping over the Obstacles that Stand Between You and Your Dream by Paul Edwards.

The McGraw-Hill Guide to Writing a High-Impact Business Plan: A Proven Blueprint for First-Time Entrepreneurs by James B. Arkebauer.

The McGraw-Hill Guide to Starting Your Own Business: A Step-by-Step Blueprint for the First-Time Entrepreneur by Stephen C. Harper.

Financing Continued Education

If you are thinking of redirecting your life through continuing education, there is a wealth of information available. Certain jobs and industries are eligible for government loans, grants, financial aid, or scholarships to help you retrain or become certified in a new career area. Other creative ideas might come to you while investigating as well. Persistence is the name of the game in finding ways to finance continuing education.

Websites

➤ www.students.gov is a site related to students and how to pay for education. It provides links to various government agencies and loans, grants, and financial aid information.

➤ Federal Pell Grants are available to those that have not gotten an undergraduate degree:www.ed.gov.

➤ www.usny.nysed.gov/grants.

➤ Check out your state's website for grants and resources as well. If you are receiving unemployment benefits, many state unemployment offices have applications available for grants to pay for tuition or to gain enrollment into training programs. Some also have small business training.

Further Inspiration for Your Quest

These are some additional, terrific books that will further enlighten your search for what's next.

What Should I Do With My Life by Po Bronson. A moving and engaging book by a brilliant writer that captures the bumps in the road and the internal struggle of forging new paths in search of finding meaning in your life and work. It is uplifting as it beautifully captures the abominable spirit of being human.

I Could Do Anything If I Only Knew What It Was by Barbara Sher. Funny and truthful, this book helps you to analyze the different reasons why you may be stuck without a vision of where you want to head in life.

Second Acts by Stephen Pollan. Very smart and concrete, this book takes you through a different process for setting a new path. It holds inspiring vignettes of famous people who have radically changed directions in their life.

Creating Your Future by Dave Ellis. This book is especially good for those that want to spend more time on the plan or need to develop the skills for following through on making the dream a reality.

General Resources

www.careerjournal.com
www.careers.org. A great resource website on alternative work.
www.workfamily.com/. Great overall work/change/balance resources.

www.employment411.com
www.careerplanner.com
www.careerbuilder.com
www.monster.com
www.salary.com

More Resources for Money-Saving Ideas

Between Friends: www.betweenfriends.org/househol.htm

BottomDollar: www.bottomdollar.com

Cash Management: Prioritizing Your Life: www.thefrugalshopper.
com/articles/cashmgt.html

Living on the Cheap: members.aol.com/Moneymstr/cheap.htm

The Dollar Stretcher: www.stretcher.com/dollar/index.htm

Frugal Family Network: www.frugalfamilynetwork.com/

The Frugal Life: www.thefrugallife.com/misc1.htm

Frugal/Mindful Living Resources: www.econet.org/frugal/

Frugal Moms: www.frugal-moms.com/

The Frugal Shopper: www.thefrugalshopper.com

A Frugal, Simple Life: members.aol.com/DSimple/

Frugal Street: www.angelfire.com/biz2/alazzia/index.html

Frugal Tip of the Week: www.brightok.net/~neilmayo/

Frugal Tips U.S.A. for Tightwads, Penny Pinchers, and Cost
Cutters: www.geocities.com/Heartland/Flats/2132/
money.html

Miserly Moms: www.miserlymoms.com/

Mothers Online Thrift Shop: www.motshop.com/

Personal and Family Finance: www.hec.ohio-state.edu/cts/osue/
famfin.htm

Right On the Money: www.rightonthemoney.org/

Suze Orman, author of *The Courage to Be Rich*: www.suzeorman.
com/resource.html
Save Big on Your Little Ones: protected.pathfinder.com/
ParentTime/workfamily/savebiglitl.html
Tight-Wadding with Doris O'Connell: pages.prodigy.com/
frugal_tightwad/

Newsletters

The Cheapskate Monthly: www.cheapskatemonthly.com
Frugal Living Newsletter: www.livingfrugal.com/
The Pennypincher Ezine: www.AllThingsFrugal.com
The Frugal Gazette Monthly Newsletter: www.frugalgazette.com

Maintaining Focus: Hiring a Coach to Keep You on Track

You know yourself. If you feel that you are not giving your all to honoring your new direction or find that life just takes over and you "don't have the time," I suggest you hire a personal coach to give structure and accountability to your transition.

For support with this 90-day process and specific, related concerns, my team of credentialed, highly trained coaches can help. To find a certified Life Blueprint™ Facilitator, contact us at:

The Life Blueprint™ Institute and LBF InterCoach, Inc.
26 Park Street, Suite 2045
Montclair, NJ 07042
(973) 857-8180
(888) 23-COACH
www.laurabermanfortgang.com

Also Available Through The Life Blueprint™ Institute:

Public *Now What?*/Life Blueprint™ Seminars

Public *Now What?*/Life Blueprint™ Teleclasses

Training for coaches and helping professionals wanting to
use *Now What?* with their clients and become recognized Life Blueprint™ Facilitators

Free quizzes and much more

To find out about the coaching profession, credentialing requirements, credentialed coach training programs, and to find other qualified coaching professionals, please check out the International Coach Federation, the largest nonprofit entity that exists to ensure excellence in the profession.

International Coach Federation
1444 I Street NW, Suite 700
Washington, DC 20005
Phone: (888) 423-3131, (202) 712-9039
Fax: (888) 329-2423, (202) 216-9646
e-mail: www.coachfederation.org
icfoffice@coachfederation.org

Send Me Your Story

Whether you used the 90-day process or came to answers before you found this book, I'd love to know your story.

Let me know how you discovered "it," ways you may have transitioned into "it," the numbers of "its" you found until you came to "it," and anything else you'd like me to know about what is making you happy and fulfilled.

Let me know how you are doing with this process, or ask questions along the way. We'd love to post on my website your stories about your 90-day results and other adventures in following your Life Blueprint. We may even ask to feature you in the paperback edition or future works. e-mail: lbf@laurabermanfortgang.com

Note to Coaches or Other Helping Professionals:

During my years as a leader in the coaching profession, I have professed over and over that coaches do not practice therapy and that coaching is about the future and not the past. This book explores the past quite often, so I would like to point out the difference between how I practice with people one-on-one and how I guide them in a written text.

In my sessions, we rarely talk about the past, and we never process therapeutic issues, but I listen for them and understand their power over an individual, so it informs how I approach the situations clients bring to me. Through my books, however, I am removing myself from the person's process, so I often include information about what I know affects them because I cannot be there myself to listen and guide them, with my questions.

Therefore, I would like to profess once again that coaching professionals are not licensed to perform therapy and don't. If the advice included here refutes that, it is only my attempt to replace myself, because the reader will not have the dialogue with me live.

My thanks to all the professionals who work to make us all fuller contributors in the world.

Acknowledgments

First and foremost, I owe a debt of gratitude to all my clients (past and present), readers, listeners, viewers, and audience members, without whom I would not be able to create this material, nor have the fun and satisfaction of assisting in people's growth and evolution. A special, huge thanks to the beta testers of this book, who made writing in 90 days fun and challenging, and who taught me so much: Thanks to all who allowed me to share their stories.

Lysa Dahlin, HR specialist, extraordinary human and good college buddy, who helped form the resource section of this book: Thanks for your expert eye and especially for the "honks." Artie Grossbard of Royal Associates in New Jersey, who reviewed and sharpened my money advice and has been a longtime personal adviser: Thanks for seeing me through from waitressing cash to today. Kevin Crawford, master carpenter and magician: Thank you for your love and the beautiful prop for this book's cover. And Arthur Cohen, my photographer for about fifteen years: I can't thank you enough for making this cover work. Thank you for your generosity and for all the great images over the years.

Joel Fotinos, my publisher, it is an honor to call you a friend. Thanks for pulling me in for another round and for the wonderful source of friendship you have become. I can already see how your introduction to the Sacred Center is changing my life. Thanks for that, too. Sara Carder, my editor, you are an angel. I can't thank you enough for making this a positive experience and for embracing my work and me so fully. You have been a wonderful guide and champion. Kelly Groves, publicity maven at Tarcher, you have made this a really fun ride. Thank you for being the inspiration for the cover and for all your enthusiasm and personal support. The Penguin sales force, Amy Halliday, Ken Siman, Kris Giorgio, Barbara O'Shea, and Ashley Shelby—it's great to be with you all again.

Joelle Delbourgo, my agent, you are as classy as ever. Thank you for being such a great source of encouragement, support, information, and friendship. You are always such a pleasure to work with, and you make me feel like I'm your only client! It's been a privilege to be included in the growth of your agency. Jenny Meyer, Carole Tonkinson, Anna Crago, Judy Piatkus, all part of the international publishing arm, thanks to all of you, new and old members of the team, for your enthusiasm and energy. I look forward to many more visits over the pond and around the world.

I have long had a mutually productive relationship with the International Coach Federation. I would specifically like to thank Bobette Reeder, Dan Martinage, Margaret Krigbaum, Guy Stickney, Kathy Shramek, Rosalind Myers, Crystal Artul-Addoh, Twana Ellis, and Sue Harford, Jilly Shaul, Elizabeth Ferguson from the UK, and all the folks in the office and in leadership roles for their support and commitment to excellence.

Friends at The Sacred Center for Living—Rod Hammer, Reverend Michael Ingersoll, Reverend Carol Logan, and all the great folks I have met doing my workshops there: thank you for welcoming me with such warmth. I look forward to our future collaborations. A huge thanks to the incomparable Reverend August Gold. You are an inspiration to me, and I am grateful for your friendship. Thanks for the longest breakfast in history.

There are so many people who have touched me deeply with their friendship and generosity in recent years. If I miss anyone in listing names here, please know that it was not intentional and that I am perhaps struck with memory loss from the deluge of love I receive. Thanks to: Carolynn Brown Turkalo, Donna Ellis, Sheila Kutner Mad Homan, D. J. Mitsch, Lorraine White, Soleded O'Brien, Jay Perry, Scott Blanchard, Ken and Marge Blanchard, Kathy and Rich Fettke, Rick Tamlyn, Jennifer Louden, Mimi Doe, Sonia Choquette, Iyanla Vanzant, Kim McCabe, Rhonda Britten, Debra Grace, Dr. Daniel Siegel, Jodi Jarel, Steve Adubato, and, most recently, Mary Ann Donahue and Samantha Del-Canto.

The team at *Redbook* magazine: What a blast it has been to work with all of you. Thank you, Janet Siroto, for bringing me on board, and to Ellen Kunes for crafting and caring about creating the perfect space for me in the book. Andrea Bauman, what a gift it is to work with you. Thank you for your care and patience and sense of humor. My thanks also to Cheryl Kramer (thanks for the trip to "the closet"), Toni Ann Paciello, Bruce Perez, Jennifer Sargent, Beth Roehrig, Jennifer Barnett, Judy Dutton, and all the folks I haven't yet met personally who work to make the column a success.

I am also very grateful to the team at Success Radio: Philippe van den Bassche, Robert Kiyosaki; Oz Garcia; Dr. Gilda Carle; Lisa Ferrari; Ed, Eric, and Steve O'Brien.

Patti Danos and Dean Draznin, two amazing PR people who

have never stopped being supportive and looking out for me even after we were officially done working together: Thank you very, very much. Eric Saxton: It will be a great ride. I have no doubt.

The team at InterCoach—there are hardly words to express how honored and humbled I am to have all of you with me. Margaret Krigbaum and Jeanne McLennan: thank you for staying the course with me. Ellen Fredericks, you have gone above and beyond the call of duty to support me, and you are an amazing friend and coach to me. Thank you. Pam Richarde, I am so honored that you've come to "play," and thanks for all our new team members. Welcome. Jeanne Bongo, managing associate and personal assistant, what would I do without you? Thank you for being there, always making it seem effortless, for being a great listener to my rants and raves, and for always having such an amazing attitude. You and your family are such a blessing.

Thanks to all the family members who take an interest in my goings-on, and especially to my parents, Fran and Bert Berman, and in-laws Joan and Morton Fortgang, for all your support. Thanks for helping us in a pinch, making vacations possible, and for being so generous of heart.

To my husband, Mark. Every year that goes by makes me feel more deeply grateful for the grace of goodness that brought you into my life. None of this would be worth it if you weren't sharing it with me. Your undying belief in me is a touchstone. Thank you. Thank you for being the juice behind so many of the projects I take on and for being the one to recognize that it was time to join business forces again. And thank you especially for being the most amazing father on the planet. You inspire me in your ability to love, your creative genius and roughhousing prowess, and your willingness to take on more and more.

Skyler, Maya, and Wyatt, thank you for letting Momma go do her work with such love and understanding. Thank you for running to greet me every day and for being the energy center of the world for me. You are amazing people, each of you in your own way, and you help me be a better person. I love you. I am so lucky to be your mom.

About the Author

LAURA BERMAN FORTGANG is internationally recognized as a pioneer in the personal coaching field and is the author of *Living Your Best Life* and the business bestseller *Take Yourself to the Top*.

As a trendsetting leader in both lifestyle and corporate forums, Laura has created work that is often featured on national television as well as in international print and digital media. Her appearances on *The Oprah Winfrey Show*, *The CBS Early Show*, NBC's *Weekend Today*, MSNBC, CNBC, CNN, and many others, combined with print media such as *USA Today*, *Fast Company*, *Money*, and many national and international newspapers, have paved the way for all of the most successful coaches in the industry today.

A popular and dynamic speaker, and one whose style translates across cultures, Laura has written books that are published in ten languages and distributed around the world. She is currently a contributing editor and columnist for *Redbook* magazine.

Through her coaching company, LBF InterCoach, Inc. Laura has provided coaching to diverse clients ranging from homemakers to celebrities and Fortune 500 companies to NASA employees and the Army Corps of Engineers.

One of the first recipients of the International Coach Federation's Master Coach Credential, Laura was a founding member of ICF and a four-year board member, and has been a tireless champion for coaching around the world.

Laura is a "Jersey Girl" and a devoted spouse and mother of three.